T0362915

PUBLISHED BY BOOM BOOKS

boombook.biz

ABOUT THIS SERIES

.... But after that, I realised that I knew very little about these parents of mine. They had been born about the start of the Twentieth Century, and they died in 1970 and 1980. For their last 50 years, I was old enough to speak with a bit of sense.

I could have talked to them a lot about their lives. I could have found out about the times they lived in. But I did not. I know almost nothing about them really. Their courtship? Working in the pits? The Lock-out in the Depression? Losing their second child? Being dusted as a miner? The shootings at Rothbury? My uncles killed in the War? Love on the dole? There were hundreds, thousands of questions that I would now like to ask them. But, alas, I can't. It's too late.

Thus, prompted by my guilt, I resolved to write these books. They describe happenings that affected people, real people. The whole series is, to coin a modern phrase, designed to push your buttons, to make you remember and wonder at things forgotten. The books might just let nostalgia see the light of day, so that oldies and youngies will talk about the past and re-discover a heritage otherwise forgotten. Hopefully, they will spark discussions between generations, and foster the asking and answering of questions that should not remain unanswered.

BORN IN 1957?
WHAT ELSE HAPPENED?

RON WILLIAMS

AUSTRALIAN SOCIAL HISTORY

BOOK 19 IN A SERIES OF 35
FROM 1939 to 1973

War Babies Years (1939 to 1945):   7 Titles

Baby Boom Years (1946 to 1960):   15 Titles

Post Boom Years (1961 to 1970):   13 Titles

BOOM, BOOM BABY, BOOM

BORN IN 1957? WHAT ELSE HAPPENED

Published by Boom Books.
Wickham, NSW, Australia
Web: www.boombooks.biz
Email: jen@boombooks.biz

© Ron Williams 2013. Reprinted 2023

Creator: Williams, Ron, 1934- author
Title: Born in 1957? : What else happened? / Ron Williams.
ISBN: 978099461575
Australia--History--Miscellanea--20th century.

Cover images: National Archives of Australia:

A1200, L17861, Albert Namatjira;

A1501, A917/2, mounted Policeman;

A1200, L22071, sandpit play;

A1200, L22359, bus queue.

CONTENTS

CHRISTIANITY IN RED CHINA	3
ABORIGINES IN THE WILDERNESS	8
TWO CHINAS	15
OVERSEAS ENTERTAINERS	19
OLYMPICS IN THE RED	29
THE LABOR PARTY AND MIGRATION	34
PROFESSIONAL FUND-RAISING	43
ONE-BRAND SERVICE STATIONS	47
FINANCING THE OPERA HOUSE	57
MUSIC FOR THE SHARKS	60
RADIATION EFFECTS	71
ARE RUSSIANS BAD GUYS?	77
ADVENT OF BILLIE GRAHAM	83
NEW SPORTS PROFESSIONALISM	89
NO-NAME GAMBLING	97
OVERSEAS TOURISTS	102
GIVE NON-BRITS A FAIR GO?	111
WE NEED AN ANTHEM	117
SPUTNIK	125
THE BEST ON THE MENU	129
10 O'CLOCK CLOSING	137
LESSONS FROM TWO ANIMALS	139
THE BODKIN CRISIS	154
SUMMING UP 1957	157

BACKGROUND DATA: Here is a page of data that will help you find your way through the book.

Queen of England	Elizabeth II
Prime Minister of Oz	Robert Menzies
Leader of Opposition	Doctor Evatt
Governor General	Sir William Slim
The Pope	Pius XII
US President	Dwight Eisenhower
PM of Britain (after April)	Harold Macmillan

WINNER OF THE ASHES:

1956	England 2 - 1
1958 - 9	Australia 4 - 0
1961	Australia 2 - 1

MELBOURNE CUP WINNERS:

1956	Evening Peal
1957	Straight Draw
1958	Baystone

ACADEMY AWARDS, 1957:

Best Actor	Yul Brynner
Best Actress	Ingrid Bergman

INTRODUCTION TO THIS SERIES

This **book** is the 19th in **a series** of books that I have researched and written. It tells a story about a number of important or newsworthy Australia-centric events that happened in 1957. The **series** covers each of the years from 1939 to 1973, for a total of 35 books.

I developed my interest in writing these books a few years ago at a time when my children entered their teens. My own teens started in 1947, and I started trying to remember what had happened to me then. I thought of the big events first, like Saturday afternoon at the pictures, and cricket in the back yard, and the wonderful fun of going to Maitland on the train for school each day. Then I recalled some of the not-so-good things. I was an altar boy, and that meant three or four Masses a week. I might have thought I loved God at that stage, but I really hated his Masses. And the schoolboy bullies, like Greg Favvell, and the hapless Freddie Ebans. Yet, to compensate for these, there was always the beautiful, black headed, blue-sailor-suited June Brown, who I was allowed to worship from a distance.

I also thought about my parents. Most of the major events that I lived through came to mind readily. But after that, I realised that I really knew very little about these parents of mine. They had been born about the start of the Twentieth Century, and they died in 1970 and 1980. For their last 20 years, I was old enough to speak with a bit of sense. I could have talked to them a lot about their lives. I could have found out about the times they lived in. But I did not. I know almost nothing about them really. Their courtship? Working in the pits? The Lock-out in the Depression?

Losing their second child? Being dusted as a miner? The shootings at Rothbury? My uncles killed in the War? There were hundreds, thousands of questions that I would now like to ask them. But, alas, I can't. It's too late.

Thus, prompted by my guilt, I resolved to write these books. They describe happenings that affected people, real people. In **1957**, there is some coverage of international affairs, but a lot more on social events within Australia. This book, and the whole series is, to coin a modern phrase, designed to push the reader's buttons, to make you remember and wonder at things forgotten. The books might just let nostalgia see the light of day, so that oldies and youngies will talk about the past and re-discover a heritage otherwise forgotten. Hopefully, they will spark discussions between generations, and foster the asking and the answering of questions that should not remain unanswered.

The sources of my material. I was born in 1934, so that I can remember well a great deal of what went on around me from 1939 onwards. But of course, the bulk of this book's material came from research. That meant that I spent many hours in front of a computer reading electronic versions of newspapers, magazines, Hansard, Ministers' Press releases and the like. My task was to sift out, **day-by-day**, those stories and events that would be of interest to the most readers. Then I supplemented these with materials from books, broadcasts, memoirs, biographies, government reports and statistics. And I talked to old-timers, one-on-one, and in organised groups, and to Baby Boomers about their recollections. People with stories to tell came out of the woodwork, and talked no end about the tragic, and funny, and commonplace events that have shaped their lives.

The presentation of each book. For each year covered, the end result is a collection of short Chapters on many of the topics that concerned ordinary people in that year. I think I have covered most of the major issues that people then were interested in. On the other hand, in some cases I have dwelt a little on minor frivolous matters, perhaps to the detriment of more sober considerations. Still, in the long run, this makes the book more readable, and hopefully it will convey adequately the spirit of the times.

Each of the books is mainly Sydney based, but I have been **deliberately national in outlook**, so that readers elsewhere will feel comfortable that I am talking about matters that affected them personally. After all, housing shortages and strikes and juvenile delinquency involved **all** Australians, and other issues, such as problems overseas, had no State component in them. Overall, I expect I can make you wonder, remember, rage and giggle equally, no matter where you hail from.

BACKGROUND TO 1957

At the start of 1957, the Baby Boom was starting to taper off. Our population of adults were starting to realise what the cause of the boom had been, and thought that it was time to have a rest. That did not mean that the arrivals at the maternity wards fell right off, rather that number slowed down from the frantic rates of the previous decade.

Happily, this slow-down did not carry over into the general economy. Instead, activity in most things was quite strong, as the many new households bought all the goodies that were needed by a burgeoning middle class. So cars were selling, new houses were being built, the enthralling new TV sets were stifling conversation, and petrol lawn mowers were turning grass into lawn. Most Dads had jobs, some Mums could find some work if they wanted it. The children were well shod, many of them wore school uniforms, and went off to State or private schools of their choice. Even the disabled or unfortunate had a security blanket of some sort that they could wrap themselves in. **In short**, our society felt secure and comfortable, it slept well at night, and it had every reason to think that, in our sheltered world, this prosperity was here to stay.

The year before, 1956, had started out that way, with only minor incidents to disturb the peace. For example, Johnny Ray, the American entertainer, flew in, unwisely on a Sunday, and was greeted at the airport by 20,000 screaming teenage girls. He was carried from the security area out onto the tarmac, his shantung suit was ripped off, his watch was stolen, and he was carried back inside saying "What happened? What happened?" over and over. He recovered, and went on to a great tour. This was one little incident that brought glee to households across the nation.

There were other events. Complaints were raised about cruelty **to** sharks (at weighing stations), Anzac Day marches were split into Catholics and Protestants, and a Tattersall's Tasmanian lottery offered a prize of 500,000 Pounds, compared to the standard NSW Government lottery prize of 12,000 Pounds. All of these stirred some passions, but not too many.

Of course, we also had some permanent annoyances that we grumbled about, but never changed. Our public transport was slow and inadequate, our country (and city) pubs were good for a many a laugh **after** you got back home, liquor reform was happening in **some** States, but not in Victoria where six o'clock closing was in force for the 1956 Olympic hordes. Then, there were strikes. Every day, the nation had a menu of **strikes** to choose from, and it was always possible to find one that met your taste. We will hear more about strikes as we proceed.

Overseas, we had two conspicuous black clouds on the horizon, but these were mainly out of sight. **The first** was the unrest in other nations. Half the nations in the world were struggling to be rid of their colonial legacies, and to reach independence. So revolutions, terrorism, coups, and local wars were occurring over half the world. Often this came down to violent dispute between white landed settlers and black poor natives. From the USA to South Africa, and in between, race riots were common, and these added to the turmoil. It was an ugly world in some parts, but we were far enough away to watch with only some interest, and no involvement.

The second black cloud was that the populated world had been divided into goodies and baddies. One group was the Capitalists, led by the Americans. The other was the Communists, led by Russia. Each of these two groups thought that it was on the only right economic track, and was prepared to kill millions of people to prove it. Already they had filled their murderous quota in Korea, would soon do so again in Vietnam, and in a multitude of other nations world-wide.

Australia was in the American camp, and so we followed the American line in international affairs. Although this was doubtless distasteful to some people, it made good sense. The reason was that we were a ridiculously small nation, with vast resources. In a bellicose world, we might tempt an aggressor who would attack us. We needed an ally. Britain, our historical protector, was no longer up to that task. America was ready to do so provided we sided with her in **her** overseas adventures. So we had given our men and aid in the unpopular-at-home war in Korea, and stood ready to do so in the future.

Still, these were not at all in the forefront of our minds at the Sunday barbecue. If we were talking seriously about anything there, it would probably have been the politics of the nation. Not that there was a great deal going on. The **Liberals**, under Bob Menzies, had been in power for six years, and would stay there for another fifteen. They were gloating the while at the dissension in **Labor** ranks, as Evatt slowly lost his edge, and as Calwell plodded towards his retirement. The main theme coming from the Liberals was that the Reds were trying to cripple the nation, and that the Labor Party was intent on giving them Trade Union support in doing this. This was a calumny, adroitly managed by Menzies in his *Reds under the Beds* jibes that were very effective electorally. More of this later.

THE BUSTLE OF LATE 1956

Towards the end of the year, four events started the tongues really wagging. **Firstly, Melbourne staged the Olympic Games**. For months leading up to mid-November, stadia and running tracks and pools and sand-pits had been created and brought to the finishing stage. Athletes had been trained, uniforms trimmed, and doves taught to fly. Melbourne's street-people and bag ladies had been **taken** away, and Chinese theatrical performers had been told not to perform in Melbourne during the Games.

Towards the end of November, everything came together in several grand spectacles, the sporting events were excellent, and the whole show passed without serious incidents. A most impressive performance that engrossed the nation and the world.

Secondly, TV broadcasts started in Melbourne and Sydney. Again, this grand adventure had been in planning for a long time, and it was completed just hours before the official opening. This was timed so that the full Olympics could be broadcast, from beginning to end, and this was accomplished without major hitches.

A number of people had bought TV sets to watch the events, and their houses became very popular for visits from neighbours over this period. The financing arrangements for buying these sets really brought into focus the **new Hire Purchase companies**, which promoted TV sets widely in the lead-up to the games. Viewers could buy a set on the never-never, even though hordes of them had a first and second mortgage. It was the beginning of the *Buy Now, Pay Later* era. In due course, a number of HP companies that cashed in on the TV boom got into terminal difficulties. You might remember Custom Credit, Cambridge Credit and H G Palmer.

Thirdly, Colonel Nasser nationalised the Suez Canal. Nasser was the Egyptian Prime Minister. Almost a century before, the British and the French had provided the money to build the Canal. By 1956, they were receiving dividends from the running of the Canal, and Nasser's Government was receiving royalties. Nasser decided that, since the Canal lay entirely within Egypt, he wanted all revenue from its operation. He announced his intention to nationalise it, and to fully take over the running of it.

Of course, this did not happen in a vacuum. He was influenced by **a lot of talk among other ex-colonial countries** who argued that they had rights to the revenue extracted from **their** assets. Basically their argument was that the nations of England and Europe had forced them into agreeing to contracts years ago, and that the time had come to abrogate these treaties, and keep their own revenues.

Britain and France could see what this meant if it was adopted throughout their former colonies. So, they moved armies around, imposed sanctions, and froze bank accounts. All the normal signs of displeasure and possibly indicating invasion.

After three months of exaggerated moves, Britain and France backed down over Suez, and withdrew all their threats, and accepted the situation. They came out of the affair with diminished reputations because they were commonly seen as using all their colonial powers to bully a smaller nation. Nasser had held steadfast throughout, and he, on the other hand, became an inspiration for other nations looking for independence.

This episode was widely reported on in Australia, especially because Bob Menzies was co-opted at one stage to lead a British deputation to Nasser. But there was no chance of changing Nasser's mind, so that Menzies' mission failed. As he limped back to Britain, the newspapers and the Labor Opposition gave him a very hard time.

Fourthly, Russia occupied Hungary. When WWII finished, Russia was able to connect a continuous ring of nations along its western border. It occupied them, and imposed Communist rule on them, and set up Red governments in all of them to create the Soviet Union. Its aim was to have a set of States that would provide a buffer against possible attacks from the capitalist states in Western Europe.

In late 1956, Poland was one of these buffer states. It tried to break away, but was quickly squashed. Hungary became infected by the same madness, and then tried to get rid of the Russians. It had no hope of succeeding. Within a few days, 200,000 Russian troops were in Budapest with 6,000 tanks.

The Hungarian opposition lasted only a week, and thousands and thousands of Hungarian men were trundled into railway trucks and sent to Siberia. Russia continued to occupy the land, and a tougher regime than before was instituted.

Most countries of the world objected to this, but there was no talk at all about effecting a rescue by force. The best that could be done was to make numerous proposals to the United Nations, but any suggestion that meant that Russia should modify its behavior was vetoed by Russia in the Security Council. So the much-deplored occupation of Hungary stayed in place until the fall of the Berlin Wall.

MY RULES IN WRITING

Before we plunge into 1957, I will explain to you a few of the standards I stick to in writing.

NOTE. Throughout this book, I rely a lot on re-producing Letters from the newspapers. Whenever I do this, I put the text in a different font, and indent it a little, and make the font somewhat smaller. **I do not edit the text at all**. That is, I do not correct spelling or grammar, and if the text gets at all garbled, I do not change it. It's just as it was seen in the Papers.

SECOND NOTE. The material for this book that comes from newspapers is reported as it was seen at the time. If the benefit of hindsight over the years changes things, then I **might** record that in my **Comments**. The info reported thus reflects matters **as they were read in 1957.**

THIRD NOTE. Let me also apologise in advance to anyone I might offend. In a work such as this, it is certain some people will think I got some things wrong. I am sure that I did, but please remember, all of this is **only my opinion**. And really, **my opinion does not matter one little bit in the scheme of things. I hope you will say "silly old bugger", shrug your shoulders, and read on.**

READY FOR 1957

So, we are ready to go. This introduction has been delivered at a fast pace, but now I will slow up and become more leisurely.

You now have enough background to go straight into 1957, and I am confident you will enjoy the trip. **Let's go.**

JANUARY NEWS ITEMS

Seventeen new Knighthoods were given by the Queen in her New Year's Honours list. Sadly, I missed out again. If you were a university professor you would have had a good chance. Or an ex-politician**. Or if you had done sterling work for last year's Olympic Games.** Still, there's always next time.

In Ireland, the **Irish Republican Army (IRA) was gaining more prominence**. On January 2nd, their para-military arm attacked police headquarters in the rural city of Brookeborough. Two men jumped from a lorry, and fired down the street with machine guns. Others lobbed grenades into the police station. Twenty policemen on garrison duty there returned fire. Two raiders were killed**. Incidents like this are becoming more common. Ugly times are ahead for Ireland.**

In Maitland, NSW, two fathers took their five children, with a packed lunch, on a picnic three miles up the Hunter River. The men as usual fished in a large pond while the children swam and walked a few hundred yards up the river. It was an outing like many before....

The men noticed that the children had got out of sight, and went to look for them. Within a few hours, the search was widened by **60 volunteers, who found the bodies of all five children in a 16-foot hol**e. Four of the children were from the one family.

Betty Cuthbert won three gold medals at the 1956 Olympics. As a consequence, the ABC selected her as Sportsman of the Year and, at the award ceremony, proposed to give her **a canteen of cutlery**. The Australian Amateur Athletics Association stepped in and advised that **if she accepted the knives and forks, she would endanger her amateur status....**

The canteen was valued at 35 Pounds. **The AAAA had an upper limit of 20 Pounds.** Instead, she was given a silver platter, valued wholesale at 11 Pounds. **Advice to you: Check the rules before you accept big gifts for your sporting achievements.**

A US rocket expert predicts that a man will be landed on the moon in 25 years. **Comment.** There is nothing in the Bible or in anything else to even suggest that this is possible. **The man is talking utter rubbish.**

The issue of **amateurism in sport** is not restricted to Betty Cuthbert. **Ken Rosewall had just made the transition to pro tennis.** He is scheduled to play Pancho Segura in 100 matches as part of Jack Kramer's world-touring pro-tennis Circus....

If Rosewall wins his series, he will be given a contract to play a similar series against Lew Hoad. But **only, of course, if Hoad turns pro later this year**. **Amateurs and pros are not allow to play against othe**r.

A new sport is attracting our young intellectuals, according to NSW Police. Young men are taking their jalopies, and heading for straight stretches of road on the edges of cities. There they **engage in the game of chicken, and drive other motorists off the road**. It is part of the culture recently imported from the USA. One lad is worried that they will run out of bombs.

CHRISTIANITY IN CHINA

The Archbishop of Sydney, Dr Mowll, was also Primate of the Church of England in Australia. Last week, he returned from a seven-week's tour of Communist China and, in a series of TV and Press interviews, made a number of statements that called into doubt the popular perceptions of Church life in China.

The picture he painted was that he met freely with many old friends whom he had known when he lived there. They told him that freedom of religion was guaranteed by the Constitution, and **it was indeed free in practise**. He pointed out that the Christian Churches were holding Sunday services, that some new congregations had been formed, and that attendance numbers were increasing. He lamented that religious schools and hospitals had been taken over by the State, but **the government did not discriminate against Christians**.

Such words were highly controversial. During WWII, the Russians and Hitler were as thick as thieves, and then Hitler, unbelievably, made the mistake of attacking Russia. So, we in Australia had to forget the 30 years of anti-Red propaganda we had been fed day and night, and instead love our new Russian ally as a brother. Then, as soon as the war was over, we were suddenly told that everything about Russia was all wrong, and that it was plainly a baddie. In fact, a very bad baddie.

So, for the last decade, our American friends had planted their unsubtle propaganda about China in our minds, and in this they were very ably aided by the Christian Churches. These latter groups were ideologically opposed to

Communism, and to the atheism that came with it. So, any incident in the world, that involved a church or its ministers struggling to live a Christian life in a Red society, brought forth immense publicity and serious complaints.

Now, we have a high ranking clergyman, a man of excellent repute, saying that the Chinese Reds were not too bad, and that they were giving Christians there a fair go. There were very few laymen, and even fewer clergymen, who wanted to give credit to this view.

The Reverend Campbell, of the Sydney Scots Church, said that Chinese Christians were free all right – as free as lions in cages. The Australian President of the World Council of Churches was of the opinion that clergymen visiting China were verging on **committing treason**.

Letters, A G Shearman. Has Archbishop Mowll lost sight of the fact that the Communists still rule in China; that they are atheistic to the core, one fundamental tenet of Communism being, "There is no God"; that they are at war with all who are not Communists; and that every act that they perform has a planned purpose and is another step in their vast scientific programme of world domination?

"They showed us everything quite freely," said the Archbishop.

Let us not delude ourselves. We can be sure that the Communists showed the delegation exactly what they wanted it to see; that they allowed members to speak only to those with whom they wished them to speak, and that they stayed and were feted only where the Communists desired.

Letters, (Dr) Fred Schwarz. The accurate assessment of public opinion is a difficult process. To identify limited personal experience with the universal situation is an error. For six years I have been touring the USA. I can honestly say that, though I have talked to hundreds of Negroes, I have yet to hear one express dissatisfaction with their conditions. It would obviously be inaccurate to interpret this as the complete satisfaction of the Negro people with their status.

The basis for the determination of public sentiment is a free and unfettered Press and free and unfettered elections. Since both these are lacking in Communist China, such statements as "the people of China seemed happy under the Communist regime" and "They feel a sense of achievement at their progress under the Communists" become the repetition of Communist propaganda.

One Letter that was **very** critical of Mowll came from a writer who said that the Chinese would have spent months preparing lies and deceits especially for his benefit, and that he had been fooled by the **actors** he had been introduced to, and by others coerced by the Reds.

Comment. Given the fact that Mowll was in China for eight weeks, it is hard to see this Letter as anything but far-fetched propaganda.

There were, of course, many who supported Mowll.

Letters, John Ryan. The views expressed by your correspondents Dr Schwarz and A G Shearman make strange reading. It would appear that, in their view, Dr Mowll, despite his eminent position and former residence in China, is too naïve an observer, and that he would be better informed if he stayed home reading the "basic texts and philosophy of Communism."

It would, indeed, be surprising if Dr Mowll hasn't already read these basic texts.

Perhaps Dr Mowll's observations can be challenged by a missionary churchman or a political observer, but one might expect that the challenge would be based not on "theoretical Communism," but on the practical experience of life in China today.

Letters, (Rev. Dr) R Davidson. Because I, too, have a profound respect for the Archbishop of Sydney, like many others, I take exception to Dr Schwarz's letter.

I would point out a fact overlooked by Dr Schwarz. Because of his many years of missionary service in China, Dr Mowll is better qualified to elicit the confidence of Chinese Christians and to assess the genuineness of conditions in their country than one who, however minutely, quotes from the safe and often antiquated pages of textbooks.

Surely visits like those of Dr Mowll and his party are to be encouraged rather than deplored in times such as our own.

Letters, Norman Paling. No one who heard Dr Mowll's sermon on Sunday morning could doubt his intellectual and moral integrity. His address was not emotional, but his voice was full of deep feeling; full of a personal love for the Chinese people which does him honour.

We may not share his religious beliefs, but we can share his humanity. Can we believe that he spent seven weeks with his personal friends of former days – much of the time quite alone with them – and did not learn something of the state of affairs?

Speech among friends is not just a recital of facts; it is a communication of emotions which give facts life. The people whom he saw around him were not strange to him; he was familiar with their lives in the past and was much more capable than his vociferous critic of judging their lives at present.

There is no religion so sacred as truth. True democracy is a struggle towards truth; a constant testing of our opinions against others, an awareness that no fact has its true meaning except in its complete geographical and historical context.

Let all those who have actual experience of life in China or a specialist's knowledge of China come into the open and give us their facts and opinions in debates in the Town Hall and elsewhere.

Many other Letters of a similar vein were printed. Thus, we end up with **two different levels of acceptance of Mowll's view**. It might best be summed up by this Letter below.

Letters, a Country Bishop. I am writing on behalf on a number of country Bishops who had the opportunity to meet recently. We cannot doubt the intelligence nor the veracity of Archbishop Mowll. **Yet we cannot doubt the oppression that is directed to the Church in China.**

We have read the claims on both sides in the Papers, and find them full of emotion and sometimes propaganda. We have realised that **we do not have the knowledge to make a judgement**, and so we can only assiduously seek, with the help of God, for the truth to be revealed in due course.

Comment. One little Letter, not I suspect from a practising churchgoer, raises an interesting point.

It said "When we survey the Christian nations during the last 50 years, with their suicidal disunity, intolerance and bloodshed, surely **it is a wonder that any Christians are allowed into China at all**."

ABORIGINES STILL IN THE WILDERNESS

In a long Letter, Ellen Kent Hughes, of Armidale NSW, presents an interesting analysis of problems associated with Aborigines. She firstly divides them into two groups. The first is composed of ordinary respectable citizens, who work their jobs, who live in ordinary houses, and whose children do well at school.

Then there are drifters, who do none of the above. As well, they drink heavily, move continually from site to site, and their children are infected with disease. Up to this point, there would be few persons who would disagree with her.

But what can be done to improve the lot of these so-called drifters? Here there are a number of solutions. Kent Hughes says that blacks guilty of repeated drunkenness should be sent to reserves and kept there for years, until they are trained to be useful in society. At the moment, she says, reserves are not used for this purpose but only to provide short-term accommodation for drifters. Their true purpose should be as compulsory rehabilitation centres, and the entire family should be incarcerated, disciplined and trained there.

She concludes with "several girls of this (neglected) type have been tried in jobs, but they are lazy, dishonest and unreliable. Even the adults have the mentality of the child. Building a few houses is not the answer; it is the character of the people that needs building up, and that takes a long, long time."

This Kent Hughes Letter reflects popular opinion at the moment. People of good will were concerned with the bad deal that the Aborigines were getting, and they would like to help them. But when it comes to the way of doing this, every person had his own hang-ups and experiences, and his own solutions.

A Mrs MacIntosh of Armidale in NSW wrote that there is a crying need for housing for Aborigines there. She calls for Associations nationwide to work toward this. Another writer, visiting Armidale, talked to natives living in humpies, and found that they "were not so sure that they wanted to live in houses." He said that they wanted to live in something they themselves had built, a cross between a gunyah and a cottage. He calls for Commonwealth control of assimilation, welfare and education. He talked about regional conferences and commissions, and advisory committees, and the advancement of the "rights of the Aboriginal." It all sounded much too academic to be immediately useful.

Another writer said that houses should be built for natives to rent, but **not in the midst of white dwellers**. This immediately brought responses that said we should avoid the segregation that was so much despised in the apartheid policy of South Africa.

There were many other Letters, each showing a different view of the problem. The encouraging point about the situation was that people were now thinking and writing about the issue, and some of these thoughts would gradually gel into actions.

Comment.   In fact, it took society another ten years of slow evolution before it took decisive action. Over this period, some wages and some living conditions were improved, and then at the end of the Sixties, various State and Commonwealth Governments made Constitutional and legislative changes that gave Aborigines a somewhat more level playing field. But, even now in 2019, no one can say that the issue has been resolved, and it remains something that, I think, the Australian people, and our Government, and our Aborigines, would dearly like to improve, but we just don't know how to do it.

Footnote. The Letter from Ellen Kent Hughes drew an angry response from another Armidale resident, Frank Archibald. He set out the nine claims that her Letter made against so-called drifters, and rebutted them one-by-one. He even added that "our characters are all right. I have 12 children of my own, and have adopted 17 others".

It is easy to understand that he could have been hurt and angry to see that his worthy life was under challenge. The fact remains, however, that most commentators at the time would agree that the Kent Hughes' Letter described quite well the vast majority of the drifters.

TWO LETTERS ON ABORIGINES

The British Government, together with our own, were again talking about firing rockets and detonating nuclear bombs in a region stretching from South Australia to the North West Cape and beyond. This had been done several times in the past few years, and always the nation was assured that it was completely safe, and no person would be harmed by it.

Always, though, there were objectors. The first of these was an inveterate guardian of Aborigines, Michael Sawtell, who for 20 years plied the *SMH* with Letters that sought to protect the black man from the ravages of the white one.

Letters, Michael Sawtell. Desert Aborigines are always starving, emaciated and without water. In that desert country right up the Canning stock route they have been the same for centuries.

You will see old gins, with legs no thicker than a man's arm, carrying loads over the hot sand. There are food and water there, but the inexperienced white man would pass them by. The water is a few feet down in secret soaks at the foot of the sand-hills, out of which only a jam tin of water can be bailed at a time.

The life of desert Aborigines is a continual hunt for food. Bush Aborigines will eat almost anything. I have seen well-fed station blacks in Kimberley eating green ants.

In the desert, if twins are born one has to be knocked on the head, and at times all newly born babies have to be killed. At all times the aged, when they become a burden, are just left to die. Go out into that country and you will see aged Aborigines who scarcely look human. What can we do about these terrible conditions?

Well, I suggest, just give them plenty of food – that is, bread and meat and as far as possible leave all bush Aborigines alone. When we detribalise and Christianise bush Aborigines, we also create other most distressing problems.

And do not forget that our Christian democracy leaves all non-exempted, full-blood, aged Aborigines to live without the pension in New South Wales.

Letters, J K O'Brien. The almost complete indifference of the Minister for Supply, Mr Beale, and the Australian public to the tragic plight of over 1,000 Australian Aborigines is a sad commentary on the state of our national conscience.

When the rocket range was established there were serious misgivings on the part of welfare workers as to the ultimate fate of Aborigines living in areas in the vicinity of these testing grounds. The select committee of the WA Parliament has revealed that these unhappy people are "living and dying under the worst conditions in the world."

Our very best people become socially conscious on behalf of the victims of Russian aggression in Hungary, while our own native race of Aborigines is destitute and dying as a result of Australia's callous neglect.

ONE BRAND SERVICE STATIONS

Some readers might remember that for a decade after the war, service stations sold many different brands of petrol. You could roll up onto the forecourt of a petrol station, and have your choice of fuel from Standard Oil, or Mobil, or Esso. From the later 1950's, this started to change, as the writer below laments.

Letters, D P Finnegan. A few weeks past, a fine dwelling was demolished to enable a one-brand petrol station to be erected opposite a well-equipped multiple station. Now, 50 yards along the same road, three fine cottages are to be demolished to make way for another one-brand station. Are we helpless to prevent such monstrous housing vandalism?

Thirty people have been de-housed to allow two petrol stations to function. Could we not ask the companies concerned to enlarge their petrol drums, allowing those evicted to shelter in the empties?

FEBRUARY NEWS ITEMS

Boydtown, a small NSW coastal hamlet just north of the Victorian border, **is for sale for 20,000 Pounds**. It includes 600 acres of land, the Seahorse Inn with 40 accommodation units, a motor camp catering for 500 people, one and a half miles of beach, and the remains of an old church, three stone whaler's cottages, and several stone wharves. **The town was the centre of whaling activity last century.**

Famous American singer, **Frank Sinatra**, was booked at the Sydney Stadium to present a seven-night series of concerts. When his tour party arrived at Honolulu, he found that his musical director had not been allocated a **sleeping** berth on the Qantas flight....

As a protest**, he returned to mainland USA**. The Australian manager of the tour has flown to America to encourage Sinatra to keep faith with his **Australian pre-paid audiences**. Failing that, ticket moneys will be refunded, he says. Sinatra has a **growing reputation of being wilful at times**.

The horse that Queen Elizabeth has ridden since 1946 slipped and fell, and dislocated his back. As a consequence, he **had to be put down**. He was a golden chestnut, and stood 16 hands high. **Buckingham Palace was notified immediately of his death.**

Last November, in a fracas between Britain and France, and opponent Egypt, **several ships were sunk that blocked traffic through the Suez Canal**. On February 10th, a neutral ship will sail through to re-open it.

In mid-month, **a widely anticipated wrestling match** was scheduled to be held at Sydney's White City Stadium, among the tennis courts there. One contestant was **giant King Kong**. The other was **Italian Primo Carnera**, an ex-world champion heavyweight fighter....

The seats were quickly sold out, and **2,000 excited Italians fought and rioted their way into the stadium**, destroying much property in the process. Meantime the match went on. It lasted for 55 minutes, and ended when the two wrestlers left the ring and stated brawling on the tennis courts. The referee declared it a "no contest"....

Wrestling (and boxing) drew large excited crowds to contests right round the nation week after week. Remember that **TV was new to the Australian scene**, so that such **live** events could still pull large crowds.

A 30-year-old man from Dalby in Queensland **bought an old car for 25 Pounds**. He took it home, and **found the sum of 25,000 Pounds in the back seat**. Police will take some time to trace it, and they think it might have been gained from war-time **black market racketeering**. If no person can prove ownership, the money will revert to the finder. **Which it eventually did.**

Famous author, **G B Shaw**, left an estate of 700,000 Pounds. He willed that it be used to finance an enquiry into the use of **the present-day 26-letter alphabet**, and the benefits that would derive from **using the 40-letter alphabet he espoused**. The British High Court ruled that his provision was not legal, and the money should go to the British Museum and the like.

TWO CHINAS

In 1949, after more than twenty years of civil war, the Communists in China finally defeated the Nationalists and were able to assume control over all of mainland China. The Reds were led by Mao Tse Tung, who over the next decades became a god-like figure. The Nationals were led by Chiang Kai Shek, and he had been propped up for years by the military might of the USA.

Chiang now retreated to the large off-shore island of Formosa (now Taiwan), and from there he beat his bare chest for many years, and became a real nuisance to the mainland government. He was still supplied by America, so his threats often took the form of military adventures, with considerable loss of life.

For decades, America refused to recognise the mainland Reds as the legitimate Chinese government, and with Australia in tow, refused it any type of seat in the UN. Formosa held the Chinese seat, despite the fact that its population was minuscule compared to that of China.

So in 1957, Australia was in an unhappy situation. It wanted to trade agriculture with China, but hesitated to do so because it was the **Red** Chinese we were trading with. Normally we could say that (somewhere in China) there was a drought, and that we could not let populations starve. Although there were always a few extremists who thought that starvation was what the monstrous Reds deserved. But wiser heads prevailed, and generally our trade deals went ahead. Still, it was quite uncomfortable, and sometimes got quite nasty as the Americans and Red Chinese used various ploys to show that one of the two could out-talk or out-muscle the other.

The Letter below addresses the Two China issue in a moderate way. It also gives some small idea that there were others issues and nations involved, and that a simple solution would be impossible.

Letters, A C Palfreeman. The time has surely come for Australia to take a progressive and constructive approach towards the twin problems of Formosa and Red China.

Australia professes to have a claim to leadership in South-East Asia. This claim does not become any more real for our attempt to sit on the fence.

The existence of the two "Chinas" should be recognised. It has become clear that the Nationalists themselves no longer look at the "return to the mainland" as a practical possibility.

We could use our influence in world councils to:-

Press the Formosan regime, with the support of the United States, to publicly renounce its claim to return to the mainland. This need in no way affect their existing defence arrangements with the United States, but could be the basis for a new spirit of independence for the island Government and an enhanced prestige for them in the eyes of the world.

Propose that the United Nations recognise the independence of the island, and eventually to substitute the United States defence agreement with a United Nations guarantee of neutrality.

Press the Nationalists to resign their seat on the Security Council, but at the same time propose that India should take its place. This involves an amendment to the Charter and needs the affirmative vote of the five permanent members in addition to a two-thirds General Assembly majority. This latter would be obtained, although it is admittedly unlikely that Russia would consent; at least her real position, vis a vis India, would be clarified.

Merely because the immediate success of any plan does not appear likely is no reason for doing nothing.

Comment. Of course, this Letter is just one man's opinion. Over the course of a month, I could have quoted you a dozen that said that, for example, the Reds were illegal holders of power in China, and that all stones should be turned until they were driven out of the nation.

OVERSEAS ENTERTAINERS

The little stir caused by Frank Sinatra pulling out of his Australian tour got a number of people talking about the value of such tours. Some people opposed these tours, because they took money away from our local artists and gave it to overseas stars. Others said the bally-hoo and wild crowd behaviour was offensive and even disgusting.

Letters, Alan Rogers. May I support the remarks of "Importer" regarding the present unrestricted importation of American so-called "entertainers" into this country.

First, as he aptly suggests, this seems hardly right at a time when dollars are at a premium for trade purposes and when all manner of restriction is being placed on the export trade – often to the ruinous loss of those concerned.

Secondly, this form of entertainment can hardly be looked upon as healthy. The screaming, the catcalling and the general wild behaviour of the audience, is anything but a healthy display.

While watching a tennis match last Friday night at the nearby White City courts, I and others round me found it difficult to concentrate on the game owing to the wild, truly animal noises from the nearby stadium. I suggest it was a real distraction to the players.

At a time when many actors and actresses have to go overseas to obtain merited recognition, and when many musicians of a superior order find it difficult to obtain a decent living, the free-go afforded to these people and the lack of restriction placed on the programmes they offer, are hard things to bear. One has only to think of the vastly superior, and infinitely more costly, entertainment being provide at the Elizabethan Theatre, and to realise the uphill struggle it is to provide such entertainment to feel extreme bewilderment and disgust at such flabbiness on the part of the authorities.

Comment. This Letter had little effect. Over the next decade, stars from the USA and Britain flooded in. Some of them were pop stars, such as Satchmo, Johnny Ray, Spike Jones, and Judy Garland. Evangelist Billy Graham made two tours ten years apart. The Beatles came towards the middle of the Sixties. Our Pommy friends sent us Donald Peers, and actress Vivien Leigh, and her husband Sir Laurence Olivier. From about 1957 onwards, artists flocked to Australia, and scarcely a week passed without some airport or stadium riot getting into the news.

DO YOU LIKE OUR OPERA HOUSE?

A few years ago, the NSW State Government started talking about building an edifice to grace the shores of Sydney Harbour. It was to be used for entertainment purposes, and would become known as the Opera House. It would be placed at a prominent part of the city, at a place called Bennelong Point, and would replace some old tram sheds falling apart there.

No one really had much idea about how much it would cost or what it would look like or how long it would take to build. Still, bravely, a number of designers were approached to create a new image for the structure. Initially it was suggested that only Australians be allowed to submit designs, but this was squashed when people started to say that we would then replace the old tram sheds with new ones.

The world-wide competition that ensued ended up in 1956 with one spectacular design, and dozens that were truly mediocre. The successful architect, Joern Utzon, captured the spirit of the Harbour with a glorious display of brilliant concrete sails that left the opposition for dead. That is, in my opinion.

Everyone, though, had different opinions. Some of them were not at all laudatory. One reader suggested that a *Big Dipper* could be placed on its roof to provide income for its upkeep. Another was worried that airline pilots would mistake it for hangers, and try to park inside. It also, we were told, looks very much like the Loch Ness Monster. Then again, "this whale of a monument to modern art will be a constant eyesore. Its over-finished roof, with many curved surfaces all covered with white tiles, will be a glaring monstrosity."

A number of readers said the money should be spent on railways, on homes, or on fixing the unemployment in the coalfields. Others said that height restrictions needed to be strictly enforced lest ugly precedents were set for the building of **future** Opera Houses.

Of course, many writers really liked the concept. The three opinions below are all in favour, but each has its own way of saying so.

Letters, Guy Lovell. Perhaps an unsuccessful competitor in the Opera House competition may be permitted to express unqualified satisfaction with the assessors' award.

Epithets like "Danish pastry, armadillo and disintegrating circus tent" spring easily to the lips of adverse lay critics, but names cannot detract from the essential merit of this design.

This merit consists in the astonishing simplicity of Joern Utzon's solution of a complex problem. How complex was the problem can, I suggest, be best judged by those who set it, those who tried to solve it perfectly, and those who made the award.

The NSW Government, trawling oceans of architectural thought the world over, cast its nets wide and wisely and had its catch expertly appraised.

That a work of the utmost architectural significance should be thus stimulated, discovered and suitably recognised reflects nothing but credit on all concerned.

How depressing, not to say humiliating, it will be if a project of world-wide interest is blocked or mutilated by any adulteration of the imagination and foresight displayed to date.

Letters, P O Miller. On a recent visit to Vienna, I asked a taxi-driver what he thought of the reopening of the opera house at a cost of £A7 million while he and remainder of 70 per cent of Viennese live in sub-standard housing with no bathrooms and with communal toilets.

He replied that, although he did not attend the opera himself, he was delighted that it had been restored as the spirit of Vienna had revived with it.

Current criticism of the proposed National Opera House project **indicates a sad lack of the cultural spirit** which is so evident in the statement of the taxi-driver. It is to be hoped that the carping critics will not succeed in preventing the erection of what must inevitably be an asset to our country, whatever the cost.

The fact that the winning design is also a masterpiece should serve as an added inspiration to those whose task it is to bring this project to completion.

Letters, Bruce Gibson. The reactions from experts, near experts and others, and the variety of opinions expressed about the winning design for the opera house at Bennelong Point need cause little surprise. **Nothing of moment has ever been done** (in this country, at any rate) **without sincere opposition**.

Many will remember the controversy we suffered over the building of the Harbour Bridge. Extending over many years the idea was resurrected by succeeding State Governments and always to meet a torrent of objections mostly on grounds remarkably similar to those now being ventilated regarding the opera house.

It was stated that a bridge would ruin the Harbour, that the cost would be prohibitive and quite beyond our ability to finance, that other works were of more importance, that it would be a "white elephant." Many, including at least one well-known engineer, predicted that it would never be successfully completed to the design as we all see it today.

When Sir Henry Parkes alienated the Crown Land we now know as Centennial Park, and set it up for all time as a play area, he was most bitterly opposed. It is indeed a strange coincidence that his son was one of the four adjudicators in the opera house competition.

When our Central Railway station was under construction at its present site, the wails of dismay easily drowned the murmurs of approval. All can still remember the knockers when Melbourne was decided as the venue for the 1956 Olympic Games.

Having allowed the winning opera house design to grow on me, I add my meed of praise for its designer, the adjudicators and the State Government, the latter for being big enough and sufficiently farseeing to sponsor the proposal. So let us to the task and may God prosper our endeavours.

Comment. Many writers said bad things about the design, and most of them added that the cost would get out of hand, and that it would take a longer time to build than the optimistic forecasts being bandied about. In the latter two respects, they were right. The cost came in many times over budget, and it took ten more years to build than anticipated.

But I think most critics at the time would **now** say it was worth it. It has become famous the world over, and is a symbol used all over Australia to promote events here. Not only that, it is a lot better place than the old tram sheds would ever have been for presenting spectacles.

Comment. You can see how I feel about it. Long Live the Opera House.

POPULATE OR PERISH

Australia had a population of about 10 million, and many of the nations near us had ten times that number and some of them had 50 times. In other words, we were small in numbers, and yet we seemingly had vast areas at our disposal. It was not surprising that people were saying that this could not go on, and that we would eventually attract the attention of some of our neighbours, and that they might even invade us and conquer us by force.

The propaganda slogan *Populate or Perish* captured this, and also the thought that if we could only go to bed full-time and breed like rabbits we could, over a period of time, build up enough infants to repel boarders. I must also be fair and say that the same people said that we should also take in large numbers of migrants to help in this regard as well. Though I add that even an extra one million persons seemed to be of little use against the hundreds of millions that were swarming to our north.

There were many different points of view on this matter. Below are three that put different slants from mine on it.

Letters, P R Stephensen. Mr Burton quotes with approval a reported statement that "we are a mere nine million Australians surrounded by 900 million Asians."

In fact, there are no Asian countries to the east, south, or west of Australia's shores. To the east are New Zealanders, to the south are penguins, and to the far west are Boers and Zulus. We are certainly not "surrounded" by Asians.

With the New Zealanders, we comprise a solid defence-block of 12 million whites in the South Pacific. We have a larger white population now than Britain had at the time of the Napoleonic Wars. Why be craven?

The time has come for Australians to discard the old colonial idea that we are defenceless against the "teeming millions of Asia." We could muster defence forces of up to a million fighting men if our country were attacked.

No Asian country, or countries, could transport a million troops to Australia in junks and sampans. A fleet of not less than 1,000 large vessels would be required to convey the invading forces and maintain supplies to them on exterior lines of communication.

Such an armada would be vulnerable to attack by our defending land-based aircraft, and by naval craft and coastal artillery – including "guided missiles."

If Napoleon and Hitler thought it not worth while to invade England, across 21 miles of Channel, what hope would an Asian Napoleon have of crossing 400 miles of the Timor Sea?

The fact is that Australians, by hard work, in 169 years, have occupied and wonderfully developed a continent which the indolent Asians neglected to occupy when it was open to them for thousands of years before 1788 AD.

When the Asians clear their abundant jungles for farm cultivation, and irrigate some of their vast open spaces – such as the Gobi Desert – they will have proved themselves as industrious as Australians; but not until then.

Letters, T A Miles. As one who has lived for many years among our nearest northern Asiatic neighbours, may I say that I have never heard from them any expressions of desire, or yearnings, to even visit Australia, much less to attack and overwhelm it.

In any case, they have sufficient troubles of their own to contend with without tackling a job which, to put it mildly, would be a "major operation."

Letters, B G Hanson. Dr Soekarno, the Indonesian President, stated on August 18, 1955: "We must free Irian (West New Guinea) with our own strength, with the Indonesian nation's own strength, and, God permitting, we **will** free Irian with our own strength (at the expense of the Dutch). Let us mobilise all our power; let us mobilise all our fighting potential."

They are now saying that they are a peaceful nation. Why has Indonesian policy on this issue somersaulted so quickly. Is it so as to completely deceive us and lull us into a state of unpreparedness?

We should strongly urge the Netherlands to fortify West New Guinea, and also take steps to build an effective defence network in that part of New Guinea **under our own control**.

Comment. Over the last 60 years, our population has increased by about 150 per cent. That includes substantial migration numbers. Most of our Asian neighbours have had growth figures bigger than that. The major exception has been China which introduced a one-child policy that still left it with large increases.

It might be that our increased population did deter invasion, though that is not immediately obvious. In any case **now**, in a different world, that threat seems to have gone away, so that if any of you are still seeking greater national security by vigorous breeding efforts, I think it is alright for you to ease back.

STAG HUNTING IS JUST FUN

In London, Sir Bernard Waley-Cohen is a member of the **Devon and Somerset Staghounds**. He, and four other members, called a Press conference **to deny allegations**

that stag hunting is cruel. He described stories of cruelty as pernicious and distorted propaganda….

Stags are "**profoundly happy when fighting to the death for a mate, and they have the same sensations in a hunt**. The animal has no forebodings of death. Hunting is in no sense cruel". The Press was not at all sympathetic to Sir Bernard's cause. One (conservative) *Times* Letter-writer made so bold as to describe it as "hogwash."

ODD BITS

Your tax rebate. Mr Sindel, of the NSW Taxpayers Association, has put the cat among the pigeons by saying that individuals **should claim a tax deduction for travel to work on public transport**. He knows that **the Taxation Department will refuse the claims**, and then his Association will challenge in the High Court. **The Tax Department says he has Buckley's chance of success**, but he is being inundated with guinea pigs wanting their "unique" situation to be argued by the Courts.

MARCH NEWS ITEMS

Peter Townsend was an Englishman **who had been employed by the British Royal family**, and who had developed **a deep and mutual affection with Princess Margaret**. Eighteen months ago there had been **talk about a marriage** between the two, and then Margaret announced that **no such marriage would occur. This was because Townsend was a divorced man....**

He was sent off basically into the wilderness and this developed into a world tour in a jeep, from which he reported his adventures. His banishment was **most upsetting to many a Brit and protests were long and bitter....**

On March 1ˢᵗ **he arrived in Perth** on his first leg of his Australian tour. The *SMH* seemed sympathetic, describing his trip as a "**lone** motor tour" and Townsend himself as "**a lone figure.**"

A few weeks ago, the NSW Education Department dismissed about **400 teachers of sewing, dress-making and needlework**. This was because of a shortage of funds, and because such **skills were thought to be of less value** than other subjects....

In early March, after much criticism, **the Government reversed this decision. Comment.** Yes it did, but not for long.

Good news for our wool industry. **Wool can now be made moth-proof.** Sounds trivial, but it really was **quite important**.

Fred Chamberlain, President of the Labor Party, opened the annual conference in Brisbane with the "**most militant speech in thirty years**." He called for the Party to **espouse a policy of socialism**, which had been slowly piling up on the dust-heap for the last decade....

Socialism now meant the nationalisation of enterprises like the banks, mines, and airlines. Ordinary citizens shuddered at the thought of these becoming **government controlled**. So, Chamberlain's speech **was seen as turning the clock back**. The re-affirmation of this policy was seen as important in keeping **Labor out of office for the next 15 years....**

Then Labor's Whitlam won office as Prime Minister, but **not on the basis of a socialism ticket**.

A **blue moon** happens every so often. If you get **two full moons in a calendar month**, the second one is a blue moon. If you get **four full moons in a season**, such as Spring, then the **third** is a blue moon. In both these cases, **the moons stay their normal moon colour**. These are predictable, and happen about once in every two years....

The other type of blue moon is much rarer and is not predictable. These are associated with **major atmospheric events**, such as a huge dust storm or the eruption of Krakatoa. **The moon appears blue**, and can be in any phase....

On March 12th, **many Sydney dwellers reported seeing such a moon**. Strangely, there was no atmospheric event that it could be tied to.

OLYMPIC GAMES IN THE RED

The Prime Minister, Mr Menzies, announced today that the Olympic Games had run at a loss as far as the Commonwealth and Victorian governments were concerned. He did not know the final figure, but he said that he had decided that the Commonwealth would pay Victoria the sum of 200,000 Pounds as its share of the loss. Victoria would have to carry the remainder.

Premier Bolte said he did not yet know the final figure, but he was sure that it would be much more than that above. Both gentlemen were quick to point out that the economic benefits that the Games had brought were well in excess of the costs, and that the taxpayer was therefore not losing out.

Comment. This argument is always put forward when a big event is held at public expense. Many people accept, too, that intangible benefits should be counted.

But others questioned whether the man in the street benefits, or is it a relative handful of merchants who do so. Certainly, it is the man in the street who coughs up the dough, and certainly it is a group of politicians who benefit from reflected glory. But, on balance, would the average citizen support the events if he realised **in advance** that there was a considerable financial cost coming to him after the bally-hoo had died down?

HOUSING FOR MOST, BUT NOT ALL

News Item. Three families, totaling 10 adults and 11 children, will be evicted from an aged corrugated-iron chook shed on the edge of the seaside suburb of Manly in Sydney. The shed is "about as long as a cricket pitch, and not much wider." It has a few holes cut in the wall for windows, and leaks "a lot" when it rains. It does have a wooden floor, but no lining, and four 30-watt light bulbs hanging from the ceiling-less roof. It has the added feature of millions of flies, and perfect ventilation throughout chilling winters.

The local Council says that the tenants will have to go, but makes no mention of where they will go to. The impoverished occupants are more forthcoming on the matter, being emphatic that they "have no place at all to go to."

There were three families involved, and two of them were from central Europe. Their sad plight raised an issue that was plaguing many in the nation. That is, the severe housing shortage, especially in NSW and Victoria. This had its origin in the early war years when governments were frightened by the prospect of inflation. They then decided to enact laws that **froze rents of all premises for the duration of the war**.

Believe it or not, those laws were still in place in 1957. Renters loved them, and landlords hated them. But the number of renters was far greater than the number of landlords, so our ruling politicians, fearful of losing votes, were reluctant to change those laws.

Thus, by 1957, housing investors were still not to be found, existing landlords were not repairing premises, and the nation's stock of livable houses was well below what was required. So, situations like the chook shed above were far too common.

Our august Prime Minister in March made a number of speeches in which he said that he was not prepared to release more government money for housing. He argued that the shortage was not caused by lack of money, but by the shortage of workers, and materials, and infrastructure, and anything else that was remotely related to building. He was not at all certain where the problem lay, but one thing was certain. His government would not be paying out any increased moneys for housing.

He managed to stir up quite a lot of comment, most of it adverse. The first writer denied that there was a shortage of material. He said that every sort of material was available for immediate delivery. He went on to say that "I dare not advertise for workers, because I would be embarrassed by the response. I could not spare the time to talk to them all."

Another writer complained the laws made it virtually **impossible to get rid of a tenant**, regardless of how badly he treated the property. And it made it almost **impossible to sell rented property**. Where else, he argued, could you watch the value of your assets decline week after week, and not have the option of selling them.

A woman complained that everything about housing was too expensive. She focused on repairs, such as guttering, and also plumbing, and said that she was appalled by the amounts that trades people charged. She, as a landlord, was not prepared to pay their exorbitant rates, and she was happy to deny repairs to her tenants. She hoped they would leave, and then she would shut up shop.

Letters, S B Hill. I am a builder of yesteryear, and some years ago I built 10 brick houses for letting, a good class of house. I have lived to regret the day I built them, all on account of the Landlord and Tenant Act.

Now, when **a tenant vacates a house** I sell. I have sold three of the 10, and believe me, sir, the money will not go back into houses.

The average man in the street recognises this state of affairs, and the older men in the industry know that private capital played a big part in providing houses for the people in the years previous to the politicians taking over and making it a political football.

The job has proved itself too big for the politician; it is time the confidence of the investing public was restored by the removal of the Landlord and Tenant Act. Until this is done, we can expect the position to go from bad to worse, with the resultant unemployment. Anyone who can't see this, can't see the wood for the trees.

A Mr Powell added an interesting insight. He, too, said that the housing shortage would persist until investors were enticed back into the market. Thus, he said, the repeal of the *Landlords and Tenants Act* was urgently needed.

He went on to say that **Western Australia had already repealed this Act**, and the normal processes of supply and demand had resulted in a good supply of houses and properties at a reasonable rental.

A builder, Mr Edwards, pointed out that there was a decided slump in building now, and that his payroll had declined by about 50 per cent. He added that 20 apprentices would be fired, and that these lads generally did not rejoin the building industry when the inevitable boom came. He called for government policies that evened out building activity, and removed the boom and bust mentality.

Letters, Gwennyth Sheen. The Prime Minister, Mr Menzies, is surely adding insult to injury in his statement that the Press is carrying a campaign of exaggeration in its presentation of the housing crisis. The victims of this crisis know full well that there has been no exaggeration, and by wilfully ignoring it, Mr Menzies is losing the support of his most faithful followers.

As a suggestion, the victims themselves have a measure of remedy in their own hands for the cost of a four-penny stamp. Every family living in crowded sub-standard accommodation, or unsatisfactorily, or who are despairing of ever getting finance, or any sympathiser who has vital facts, should write at once to their Federal Member giving briefly these facts. From this cross-section a clear picture of the situation could be gained.

Letters, Dr A H Sheehan. As a practitioner who visits the homes of families in supposedly garden suburbs, I was disturbed by Mr Menzies's statement on the housing problem.

It is typical of the word-play of many of our politicians, both Liberal and Labor. It serves to confuse an issue which is vital to the happiness of our country – we want and need houses quickly.

If our so-called leaders do not know that many families are living in unhygienic, cramped rooms – sometimes a family of five to one room – then they have lost touch with reality.

This letter has been prompted by a visit to a child with rheumatic fever, one of six living in a damp, unhealthy room – this visit was one hour after I read Mr Menzies's fanciful address.

By the end of the month, Letters were still coming in. One suggested that costs could be cut by reducing the mandatory ceiling height, and by allowing the use of timber and tin instead of the sometimes requirement for bricks and tiles. A good washing machine within the house could replace the laundry.

A few writers pointed out the incongruity of older people - because of Government restrictions - being worried sick about the expense of keeping homes that are too large, while younger people are worried about bringing up their children in overcrowded conditions. "Oh for some honest-to-goodness common sense."

Despite this deluge, Menzies remained adamant. This was unusual for him, because he was normally very perceptive of public opinion, and swayed when the pressure became obvious. Of course, he knew he could get away with his Scrooge-like refusals, because he was under no pressure from Labor while Evatt and Calwell were its leaders.

So, the travesty moved on, and nothing changed. A few of the States nibbled away at the various *Landlords and Tenants Acts*, but in NSW and Victoria in particular, nothing changed for another decade. So, for 25 years, from about 1942, tenants had their rents fixed, and landlords also had their receipts fixed.

I go back to my earlier thought. Can you believe that?

THE LABOR PARTY AND MIGRANTS

In the dozen years since the end of the war, about a million migrants had come to this country. Almost all of them were from Britain or Europe, and many of them had only basic skills.

The local trade unionists, and the Labor Party, had mixed feelings towards these good people. **On the one hand**, they believed, as did the nation, that we must "populate or perish". This was the theme that said we were vulnerable to attack from overseas because we did not have the manpower to protect ourselves. So that every migrant was welcome because his presence here meant that we were better able to resist invasion.

On the other hand, in a nation that was crying out for more and better housing, the influx of migrants meant that competition for houses was increased, and that meant that some existing residents would miss out. The same was true for jobs, and here it was the unions and the Labor Party that were most vocal of the dangers of admitting more migrants.

So, the matter was argued at length back and forth. Now a migrant added his voice to the cacophony.

Letters, Karel Svoboda. This is my personal experience: Born in Czechoslovakia, I came to Australia from Europe more than eight years ago and have since acquired Australian citizenship. At the time of my arrival I was practically penniless but determined – as most migrants are – to work hard and establish a new home and family here.

My first job was in a huge factory. As a migrant, I was naturally given the dirtiest job in the factory – as I was told the union would otherwise object.

Very soon the local union representative, who professed – and very loudly so – to be a Labor man, invited me to join the union, **or else**. Whereupon I joined the union.

From the start, I was looked upon by the other union members as a queer bird. My aim was to work hard and long and to use the money earned for my future.

Their aim was to work as little as possible, to go to races and drink beer.

Every free minute I had, I spent learning English, and the customs of this country.

After a few months in the factory it was clear to me that despite my qualifications, I would never be able to get a better job, because of the union and the peculiar attitude of its members who regarded my striving for better future through hard work as utterly un-Australian.

I also came to the conclusion that the only solution was to buy a small business of my own where I would be my own boss. Also, I realised that the Australian Labor Party, far from being a party promoting social justice and a fair deal for all, appears to be a party of the lazy man. Do little work, work slowly, abuse the boss. That seems all that there is to it.

Why should any migrant conform to such policy? All this quite apart from the often open hostility shown to him by his fellow-workers. Even the official organs of the Labor Party seem to bring it home to every migrant that he is an unwanted stranger and a second-class fellow. Why should he then be enthusiastic about the other aspects of policy of that party?

Labor supporters were quick to claim that there was another side to the picture.

Letters, Frank Vanry. Karel Svoboda's letter is one of the many generalisations and misrepresentations which do only harm without contributing anything to mutual understanding.

I for one had exactly the opposite experiences. Since arriving in this country 18 years ago, I worked in seven workshops and factories of various size, from six to 800 employees. To my great surprise I was not once approached by union delegates or fellow workers about my membership if I did not contact them by my own free will.

As for the laziness or otherwise of the Australian worker. He is as good or as bad as any in the six countries I know. Many of them are very proud and satisfied to do a good job properly – others look at work from a different angle. But I had **the same experience with the representative of management**. Some of them were efficient and able to get the maximum out of man and machine; the others were spoiling both by misleading.

Where on earth would Mr Svoboda find a country where, after arriving penniless, he could in eight years be his own boss and own a business by "doing the dirtiest jobs only." And how much of this does he owe to the Australian Labor movement in general, the trade-unions in particular? By their struggles in the past and their solidarity at present, they protect the worker from being lowly paid.

So, at this point, the score was one all. Then another writer introduced another element into the fray. He talked about Labor's links to the Communist Party and, learning from Bob Menzies, smeared Labor with a Red haze.

Letters, H V Bloem. One of the main reasons why migrants come to Australia is to be as far as possible from Russia and her Communism.

And now in Brisbane we are called fascists if we do not vote for the ALP. **But what is the so-called ALP doing?**

The leader of the ALP, Dr Evatt, defended Communists in Court and did everything possible in the Petrov case to defend the Communist view. He even wrote to the Russians for support of his views. What other answer could any sane man expect than that the Russians would deny any connection with Petrov's activities.

As long as the so-called ALP has not the courage to go it alone with their own ideals, regardless of the Left-wing members, who call themselves Labor but are in reality Communists, a majority of the New Australians will not vote for the Australian Labor Party.

Finally, **these** few considered words might have contained a fair amount of wisdom.

Letter, Jim Comerbank. I have worked on industrial sites from the end of the war right up to the present time. I have seen the migrant Poms come in, followed by the Poles and Balts, and then the so-called skilled workers from Britain and Europe.

There can be no doubt that some migrants were given a hard time by local workers, just as some migrants at times were welcomed with open arms. It might be a platitude, but it seems to me that if a migrant entered the workforce with an open mind, and was prepared to accept initially some Smart Alec jokes at his expense, then he readily gained acceptance. On the other hand, if he did not roll with the punches, the road ahead for him was a hard one.

GHEE

Ever since reading your Rudyard Kipling, I know you have been waiting for some news on ghee. These few Letters will bring you up to date.

Letters, (Mrs) C Brown. I have used butter treated the ghee way for more than 25 years and find it better for all cooking than fresh butter. You will find many country women treat their surplus butter in the same manner.

I do not seal and have found it to keep fresh for 12 months.

Letters, T G Corden. Your correspondent's recent article on the possibility of ghee being marketed here prompts the query, "Why?"

Having for a period of years been compelled to use this product in India and Persia, I feel confident that the sensible Australian housewife will consign this vile-smelling (when cooking) and nasty tasting product to its rightful place, i.e. – the garbage tin.

Letters, (Mrs) E M K Johnson. I am an ardent user of ghee and find it is unsurpassed for its cooking uses and food value. We should welcome the marketing of this product, knowing that it is manufactured from pure creamery butter from our own Australian dairy cows.

Ghee has no smell or disagreeable taste.

Comment. I hope the matter is now clarified.

NEWS AND VIEWS.

Horses first. Letters, E R Williams. At 8.15am on Friday at the south-east entrance to the Show-ground, I saw a restive horse being held up by a traffic policeman to allow private motorists to proceed on their way.

At this time of the year, when many country horses, unused to heavy traffic, are in the city, it should be brought to the attention of the public, and police (if it has not already been done) that the law requires all motor traffic to give way to a restive horse. It further lays down that, if necessary, the motorist must come to a complete halt and cut his engine.

A BUILDER'S INTERESTING COMMENTS

Letters, W Edwards. The building industry needs assistance from engineers, technicians, and industrial chemists who have provided a number of synthetic materials which can be cheaply produced, and which do not possess the defects of present building materials. A modern house still consists of one-third timber in spite of all defects of wearing and shrinking. There is no reason why steel should not be used for joists and rafting in fibro-constructed houses. The whole frame, including the roof, could be of fabricated steel. During the twentieth century, almost all the large industries have been re-organised, but not so with building.

Engineering mass production methods are essential if we are to lower costs. In the Ford Willow Run Factory, huge bombers came off the line at the rate of one per hour – why can't we organise the engineering industries of this country **to produce a house per hour**? It can be done if the resources were utilised to that objective.

Steps should be taken to modernise the brick and tile industries, which are 50 years behind the times. We should instal modern excavators and conveyors instead of picks and shovels and trucks pushed by man-power. We smile at the Arab's plough, but brickyards are just as ancient. Why do builders and Government authorities **insist on building houses to last three to four generations?** Compare the motor car of today with one 20 years ago. The engineers have given us a greatly improved car at a lower cost. The chaotic state of housing will not improve until modern engineering methods of production and planning are adopted right throughout the entirety of all the building industries.

APRIL NEWS ITEMS

Jervis Bay is a well-known town on the southern part of the NSW coast. It has 58 permanent families as residents, but is **flooded with visitors during school holidays**....

The Navy wants the area to establish a naval base. So all occupants must **leave the township by September**, and businesses are already closing down. No provision has been made to relocate the 300 people affected. Long-term locals are not happy. "We were born here 60 years ago, **where can we go that's as good?"**

It was thought by the Government that the nation's defences were not adequate, so that **in 1952 it introduced Bills that required all young men to enter the Army for National Service**. This meant that at 18 years of age they were taken from the loving care of their families, and were put into big camps under the equally loving care of our national military authorities....

There they learned to fire guns and grenades, stick bayonets into hessian bags filled with grass, and how to shine and blanco their military issue, and to salute....

I was one of the lucky lads who did my three months initial training. **It was, to me, a great rort**, full of the fun to be had by quietly bucking authority, and **at the same time learning some very useful skills**. Despite the absolute futility of it all in terms of defending the nation, it did turn a rabble of silly young men into a rabble of slightly disciplined and **mostly better** silly young men. In April, the government announced that **it**

would terminate the scheme. **Comment.** The scheme did not achieve its purpose at all, but it was worthwhile in producing better citizens.

A prominent US physicist predicted that **ocean levels would rise 40 feet within the next 50 years**. Dr Kaplan, of the University of California, said that the burning of fuel was the culprit, and it would result in **the melting of ice caps** near the Poles. The oceans would roll through **the streets of New York, London, Sydney**, and other coastal cities....

Does this sound familiar to you? **It is now 60 years since that prediction**.

The Federal Government has decided that the nation's defence capabilities will be strengthened if **we build our own planes**. Thus, they announced plans to **build a 2,000 miles per hour Starfighter Jet**, based on American prototypes.

Comment. Neither the plane nor the proposed new industry got off the ground. Sixty years later, we buy our military planes and big passenger jets from America or Europe.

The City of Sydney authorities said that it planned **to remove more fruit barrows from the inner-city area**. This was consistent with other cities round Australia....

One reason to do this was to improve **traffic flow** in the cities. Also, some people argued that hygiene at barrows was poor, that **the horses that pulled them were badly treated**, and that the barrow-men were deceptive in putting good fruit at the front, but serving from the back.

FUNDRAISING IN THE HANDS OF PROS

A number of Protestant churches were running short of money. So they adopted a fund-raising approach that was currently working well in America. This involved the sending out of well-trained **advocates to the homes of parishioners, and basically asking for money**.

Of course, it was not as blunt as that. The advocates were themselves parishioners, who were trained by the overseas advocates. Each of them was given a quota of houses to visit, and after gaining entry on the basis of a common interest in a church, quietly conversed until the parishioner saw fit to make some kind of on-the-spot donation, or promised to do so in the future.

The promise might just be that they would attend church services and donate to the fund. Or give money for a building. Or buy tickets for a Ball, or a group of orphans. Richer donors might promise to finance some larger project, and perhaps have their name emblazoned somewhere. Regardless of the sum collected or promised, the basis of the approach was that it was God's will that every person should contribute, and it was part of the divine purpose that such gifts be made. The visitors came with a wealth of biblical quotations that spoke well of their cause, and it was hard for the ordinary unsuspecting church-goer to say no.

There were a number of parishioners who became restive as the various campaigns gathered strength. Then one of them, a pastor from the Church of Christ, spoke out.

Letters (Pastor) A C Caldicott, Church of Christ. A Melbourne paper recently carried an advertisement in large print "Top Flight Executive Wanted For Church Organisation," mentioning a firm of high-pressure salesmen noted for their fantastic but apparently successful methods of extracting finance from church-goers and non-church-goers. There were no qualifications necessary except that the applicant had to be a "Top Flight Executive." Be he believer or non-believer, temperate or otherwise, this was seemingly of little importance; it was the business acumen that mattered most.

Churches must have finance in order to fulfil their task of preaching the Gospel, but let it be known that **God is no beggar** and never intended His servants to be. However, present-day finance methods, operating far and wide in this land of ours, find representatives of the churches standing on doorsteps which have never been darkened by Christ's ministers for years. **Their mission? Solace, comfort, concern for souls, a ministering word? No, the mission is to solicit money!**

Each Christian decides for himself what he shall give – "as he purposeth in his heart." He does not give as the financial secretary decides for him. He does not succumb to tricks, schemes, devices, or pressure tactics. He gives freely and willingly, because he loves the Lord.

Anything that a Christian gives unwillingly may help someone else, but it certainly does the giver no spiritual good. Contributing of money to God's work should never be done in the spirit of payment of a debt.

The well-known Rev Gordon Powell, of the Presbyterian Church, was quick to respond. He labeled Caldicott's letter as unkind and uncharitable, and pointed out that the US organisation his church was using "applied no pressure, and certainly were not salesmen." The actual visits were all done by parishioners. The philosophy was that each should give according to his ability, both the rich and the poor. The widow who gave her mite shared with the congregation the joy of giving to God. "To all who have caught this spirit, a new spiritual experience has come."

Other writers had their say.

Letters, (Rev) Richard A Engel. First, the volunteer canvassers: These men are described by the pastor as "pressure salesmen." He describes their work as soliciting money, and denies their concern for souls, for the offering of comfort, solace or a ministering word.

Our men were not like that. They were specifically trained not to be like that and, indeed, few of them would have volunteered for the task if it was to be high-pressure or unspiritual. They went out somewhat warily, thinking that perhaps people would not accept what they had to say because it aimed so high. The aim was always a sacrificial, humble, willing and generous gift.

They came back enthused. They found that their words were "ministering words." They were accepted by the congregation as bearers of religious truth concerning giving. That their mission did not often touch on their aspects of the Gospel was accepted by them and by the people to whom they went, but they still came back communicating their concern for the spiritual welfare of the people to their minister. They were out scouting for their pastor with open eyes for cases of spiritual need. This was of tremendous value to me, to the people, and to themselves.

Second, the big-amount givers: Pastor Caldicott seems to have a prejudice against such people simply because they are not only able, but also willing, to give big amounts.

I have found that the big-amount givers to our church were not only humble but extremely conscientious about their gifts. Even the widow with her mite – and we had plenty of these generous folk, too – gave credit where it was due and received credit.

In my opinion the only loss by these canvasses is to those **who do not take the occasion to examine their giving in the light of spiritual truths**. The occasion is presented very clearly. Even the pastor can be awakened to the necessity of giving more generously.

Several other Letters all said that Pastor Caldicott was not seeing the position correctly, and many of them threw up their hands in horror at the thought that they were condoning the methods of debt collectors. Then the good Pastor put his case succinctly and perhaps even better than his original Letter.

Letters, (Pastor) A C Caldicott. While Church authorities applaud the raising of close on £8 million in a remarkable short space of time, it needs no master-mind to calculate the **amount of money that goes to the firm of enterprising businessmen and eventually overseas to America**.

No doubt all the Church groups participating are sincere in their programmes calling for increased giving, but there are the rights and wrongs to be considered. It is not right that any firm of businessmen should use the Church as a source of income.

Of course, from the point of view of Church boards and minsters, it is a relief to sit back and know that for a time, financial worries are at an end, but the machinery set in operation, and legitimately so at that, savours something of the legitimate dealings of the money-changers in the Temple.

It is somewhat idealistic to hope that gilt-edged invitation cards, loyalty dinners, and financial appeals can effect a change of heart in the rich man. Fund-raising schemes were never intended of God as the means of conversion. God wants the heart first, not the money.

Comment. At this point, the Editor closed the discussion.

SUPER FOR POLICEMEN

In 1957, most workers did not have to worry about their superannuation, simply because they did not have any. Public servants **did** generally have super schemes, and were lucky enough receive a modest pension upon retirement. This applied also to the employees of the really big corporations and big institutions. But **most workers had no provision at all**, and generally relied on the old-age pension, provided that they could pass the assets test.

Employees who **were** superannuated were forced to make deductions from their pay to cover the cost of their scheme. But apart from the pension at the end of their service, they could expect to be paid out some portion of their accumulated super **if they left work early**. Of course, the employee who worked for life at a single job did not have to worry about this. Still, it was nice to know that if they left early, for whatever reason, they would get some super back.

But now it came to the notice of the public that this was not true for all public servants. In NSW, and elsewhere as well, one body of worthy workers were excluded from this benefit.

Letters, K Roberts. The Police Superannuation Act makes no provision whatever for resigning or dismissed members to receive **moneys which they have subscribed from their own personal earnings**

to the superannuation fund. This is tantamount to misappropriation of private funds and nothing less.

A greater injustice cannot be imagined when a policeman, with an honourable record, is not granted money deducted from his own personal pay cheque when he desires to resign and possibly improve himself in life.

And how useful would such money be to a dismissed policeman who is charged in the court with an offence when he has to battle to raise funds for his defence to clear his name.

The *SMH* added a few facts. It noted that police had 4 per cent taken from their weekly pay to cover the scheme. Also, that **every year** the Police Association annual conference passed a resolution to the Minister for Police pointing out the anomaly, and that nothing had ever been done to remove it.

It went on to say that denial of superannuation fund repayments to men who leave the New South Wales Police Force by resignation or dismissal is an incredible piece of injustice. Almost as incredible is that it has been allowed to persist for so long. It would be difficult to find another body of Public Servants who are so harshly treated. Certainly the practice in ordinary business organisations with contributory superannuation schemes is to return to a contributor his own payments on resignation.

Another ex-policeman spoke in practical terms.

Letters, William Wood. In 1947, with 20 years' service, I resigned from the NSW Police Force. I forfeited approximately £200 – the total of compulsory super deductions taken fortnightly from my pay during my service. After interest, that sum would now be £300.

Many other ex-police have also suffered similar financial loss, to a greater or lesser extent. The total of money filched in this way would doubtless shock any fair-minded person. Police have often protested, but the injustice remains. Mr Roberts is correct – no similar position exists elsewhere.

Comment. I do not need to drone on about the injustices here. I will though remind you that much needed reforms to the super system have been very slow to come. Indeed, 60 years later, there is still much to be done.

Personal comment. I have seen many dodgy practices over the years as super has become an industry in its own right. For example, I have seen men sacked a year before retirement so that the employer could pay out only half the members' contributions. On the other hand, I have seen public servants given big rises in status and salary just before retirement in order to benefit their pensions.

In the 1970's I had a friend who worked and contributed for almost seven years, but then left his job. He got none of his super back, and then, a year later, was dunned for a levy to pay the debts that the fund had run up.

Still, **the growth of super to every man and woman has been one of the big stories of this last 60 years**. One feature has been that every serious employee has a substantial sum taken from his pay packet each week, and **that money is invested on his behalf**. So every worker **is now a capitalist**, and this applies to everyone, from the bloated bankers to the most radical shop-steward on the factory floor. **A big change over the years. I wonder what Karl Marx thinks of this.**

ONE-BRAND PETROL STATIONS

After the war was over, petrol rationing was suspended. Mind you, it took five years to reach that happy state, so it was not until 1950 that the newly elected government of Bob Menzies made the popular move.

By then, local garages in towns and suburbs had fallen into disrepair, and were badly run-down. For years there had been little petrol to sell. Further, the car-repair business, that went hand-in-hand with selling petrol, had dropped toward nil because there were few cars on the road. At the same time, because the owners now had a very precious and scarce product to sell, namely petrol, they often exalted in that position, and dictated who would be able to convert their precious coupons into petrol. In short, any form of civil customer service was hard to find.

In the mid-fifties, the big petrol companies decided to change all that. They campaigned at government level for legislation that banned petrol stations from selling **multiple** brands of petrol. Up till now, most garages in the nation had **two or more different branded pumps on the forecourt**, and the motorist nominated which brand he wanted. Of course, they were all selling exactly the same product, but still each driver had one particular brand that he was prepared to argue for.

Now, however, the big companies agreed that the industry needed a shake-up, and that they were prepared to finance it. But they wanted to have full control of their sites, and not share them with lots of their competitors. Thus, they pumped out their persuasive propaganda to governments and the people, **they wanted one-brand service stations**.

And, they added in brackets, they wanted to be rid of the repair businesses, and become just sellers of petrol. And they wanted legislation passed so that multi-brand stations would be banned and **only single brand stations would survive**.

So, in 1957, the battle for these new premises was on. The companies were buying up hundreds of new sites round the nation, and promising that the terrible services given by the old owners would be replaced by spectacular new driveway services and fast attention to motorists needs.

We take up the story with the mild Letter below..

Letters, C Dean. Many car-owners buy petrol and oil at one garage, but take their cars to other garages for repairs – inconvenient no doubt, but necessary because the first garage sells the desired petrol but does unsatisfactory repair work, while the second has the wrong petrol but does have the client's confidence regarding repairs.

If the oil companies are sincere in their claims that they wish to tender better services to motorists, they might organise their representatives throughout the Federation to question motorists to discover whether the latter are satisfied with one-brand stations, or would prefer a return to the multiple-brand service which existed before.

The NRMA added a bit more information to the debate that was developing.

Letters, H E Richards, General Secretary, NRMA. Prior to the survey, the association had been advised by oil company representatives that their service training required the filling station attendants to reach the car quickly upon its arrival, courteously greet the client and, without request, clean the windscreen and check oil and water; the checking of batteries and tyres was not included in automatic driveway service, but was available free if requested.

The writer below asks a few questions of Mr Richards.

Letters, Cecil de V Hardcastle. Mr Richards should be aware that there is no such thing as a "free" service, and that his association would be better employed in fostering a spirit of self-help in such matters as the cleanliness of windscreens, etc., and leave the service station man free to sell petrol and oil promptly, as well as to render those needed services to motorists in trouble, which I, for one, have always found them ready and willing to give.

This Letter below looks at the controversy from a retailer's point of view.

Letters, C A Gregory, Service Station Assn of NSW. Motorists generally (nature being what it is) expect as much as possible for nothing, though they have been especially "educated" to look for hand-outs from service stations that they would not dream of getting from any other class of retailer.

The giving of all the free services listed above occupies about twice as much time and Labor as does the serving of four gallons of petrol – the average sale on a station. Thus two-thirds of the time of the attendant may be taken up for no return.

While the motorist likes to be at the head of a queue for free service at any station, he will, with the impatience typical of most car-owners (and the writer is one of them), pass a station on which other motorists already are on the driveway for free service. Thus, in giving this service, a motor trader loses directly by providing, **for nothing**, much that costs him something substantial in labour, plant, and materials; and indirectly by frightening away potential customers who by-pass him while he is engaged in his give-away activities.

Of course, the big suppliers had something to say.

Letters, G Geddes-Wrights. I feel that the NRMA should be the last to encourage that small-minded type of motorist, who, having little to do at the moment, proceeds to the garage, has a gallon or so of petrol, and then does his best to block everyone else by grabbing as much of the so-called "free" service as he can. If a charge of 1/ per tyre were made, this type of pest would be largely eliminated.

As for suggesting that someone clean one's windscreen – this seems to me to be foreign to our way of thought.

One final Letter hits the nail on the head.

Letters, R F Winson. How many of us have forgotten those wartime days of shortage when one cringed hopefully to one's retailer for some badly needed commodity? When things were in short supply what sort of service did we get?

Remember the curt refusals, the studied ignorance, the "you're lucky to get it" attitude? When cars were hard to get and customers were queuing up – remember the attitude?

Good luck to the one-brand stations in their efforts to improve service to the motorist; in fact, good luck to every businessman who genuinely tries to improve service for his customers. It is to that man that my patronage will always go, and I am not alone.

Comment. As we all know, the "little guy" lost **this** battle. He limped along for another twenty years, and then was gone. Apart from the economics of having a single provider and better services, the old owners had built up big resistance to themselves during the 15 years of slack and preferential service. This is seen in the last Letter.

On many occasions, the "corner store" operator gets a great deal of sympathy from the general public, and some of these survive even against the giants who now dominate. Not so however, for the old owners of garages. They lost general community support a long time ago, and when this battle for turf started, they had few friends.

HAIRDRESSERS DIVIDED

One Hairdresser's Union was advocating that **shops be allowed to open one night a week** so that women could get **their hair dressed**. It said that working women could no longer get to hairdressers and as a result their hair was ungroomed, unsightly, unshaped **and no longer their crowning glory....**

Another Hairdresser's Union was opposed to late-night closing because hairdressing was an **"intricate and artistic job, and is hard on the eyes**. After a worker has done eight hours, he has had enough."

MAY NEWS ITEMS

During the running of the Albury Cup, three horses and their jockeys fell. **One jockey was killed, and two others were critically injured.** One horse died instantly, and another was destroyed.

The new game of *chicken* is gaining popularity among our young warriors of the road.

The Australian play *Summer of the Seventeenth Doll* opened in London, and had been booked to proceed to the US. In London, the cast was Australian, and was described by a critic as **"worthy rather than satisfactory"**. The story was described as "dull, flat and unrevealing." The play had been a huge success in Australia. When it went to London it was described **as heralding a new age for Australian theatre overseas**....

I saw the play before it left these fair shores, and my comment in a letter to home was that **it had "a lot of shouting people in it",** and that it was not worth going to Newcastle (30 miles) to watch it.

The grand concept of an Opera House for Sydney was causing much friction. Opponents were saying that it would take money away from schools and hospitals and roads, and that the State of NSW could not afford it. There was a lot of talk about **running a series of lotteries to finance it**. There was also a lot of talk about **scrapping the whole project** and rebuilding the tram sheds on the site. At the moment, there is **an even-money chance that it will not go ahead**.

The sport of soccer was in the news constantly. It was a growing sport in Australia as lots of migrants flooded to our shores. But it was not the games that got the sport into the newspapers. It was **the conduct of the crowds....**

Most of our teams were based round a particular nationality. So when two teams met, **the animosities that existed in Europe** showed up again at the soccer, and punch-ups and riots were common. **These were getting the sport a bad name.**

The Beach Broadcasting Company is approaching Councils around the nation suggesting that it be allowed to **play music from loudspeakers across their beaches at weekends.** For a fee of one shilling, a customer could request a three-minute tune, and that would be **followed by a one-minute advertisement....**

Coolangatta had already adopted the system, and major **Sydney Councils are discussing it. Churches oppose it** because it would desecrate the solemnity of Sundays. The Company hopes to have it installed **on 90 per cent of the nation's beaches soon.**

The Federal Government Health authorities have come to the conclusion that **there is a link between heavy smoking and lung cancer.** They are advocating that the Government start **publicity campaigns** to encourage people to smoke less. They point out that smokers of ready-made cigarettes were equally at risk **as were roll-your-own users of tobacco.**

FINANCING THE OPERA HOUSE

Australia is a big country, with a small population. It had a high standard of living in 1957, and it wanted all the amenities it could get. But there was little agreement on what these were. One suggestion was that we wanted a splendid new opera house, and plans were already being made to build one. But not everyone agreed that this was our **first** priority.

So, the NSW Premier, Joe Cahill, was thrashing round trying to find ways of financing his dream project. This was not the time for raising taxes, and many alternatives were suggested. One of these was to run a series of lotteries. You can imagine how much opposition that idea ran into, especially from the Protestant churches. Raising money from gambling? Surely not.

So Cahill, with a convincing display of on-again-off-again politics, went into stalling mode for a few months. Meanwhile, Letter-writers were sharpening their quills.

One batch of writers resisted lotteries on moral grounds. For example, "gambling is vile, second only to alcohol in grip and destructive effect, and more subtle in onset. No plea of expediency or profit can make a government which fosters this vice anything other than vicious."

Another batch of writers were happy to offer alternative uses for any money that could be found. Of course, hospitals and roads and education were often mentioned. "**School buses** are doing a gigantic task, and are finding it difficult to keep going now that subsidies have been reduced." Then there was a suggestion that if a lottery were held, the prizes should be 20 houses each valued at 25,000 Dollars, instead of the suggested 500,000 Dollars.

Others, however, had different views.

Letters, Warwick Jensen. The opera house controversy seems to me to have reached almost absurd dimensions.

Why not face the cost squarely, all of us, and put our individual mite abstractly into the cause of culture so necessary and important in any nation?

As an individual in the £1,000 a year income bracket with a family to keep, I would cheerfully pledge myself to donate £5pa for such a worthy cause. Mr Cahill, and probably thousands, feel the same.

By all means build houses as well, as I am in the process of doing now.

Letters, Harry Neate. It is difficult to follow the horse and buggy philosophy of opponents to the building of the opera house now.

The opera house or national theatre is undoubtedly a pressing need. Such a building would be evidence of maturity. The international prestige would be worth millions in advertisement for Australia.

Mr Cahill is to be congratulated on the proposed method of financing this undertaking. His plan has the following advantages: (1) The lotteries will collect money that can be afforded – at least, willing subscriptions.

(2) The proceeds will include a large percentage of money that the working man or woman can give to a good cause (with a remote chance of good fortune) rather than to idle bets at SP or frivolous amusement.

(3) It does not depend on the funds intended for housing, hospitals, education, public works, etc.

(4) Probably 90 per cent will consist of money that would otherwise go to bookmaker, brewer, or "business."

(5) It allows many to support an imaginative man with a plan of great national importance.

Letters, Ann Young. Sydney is fast growing into one of the world's great cities and should have an opera house worthy of itself.

However, it would be completely wrong to use Government funds, State or Federal, for such a project, when two most important things are in short supply, viz: housing and education.

The majority of country people will take a very dim view of millions of pounds being spent on a city building, when they are desperately in need of roads, transport, electricity, measures to alleviate fires, floods and drought and many other things too numerous to mention.

Sydney is a rich, very rich city and the people are generous and should be given the chance to wholeheartedly donate the money before resorting to Government money or monster lotteries.

There may be only one person who could give £100,000 and perhaps two who could donate £10,000 each, but surely there would be in this city 200 people willing to give £1,000 each and 2,000 people who would give £100 each and so on right down to the widow's mite and the school child's shilling.

Only through giving can the opera house be a spiritual achievement to add to this proud city of ours.

Letters, C S. Merely as a matter of interest, and without wishing to take sides in the controversy now raging round the proposed opera house, may I mention that the British Museum was started with a lottery?

Comment. Despite all the logic, and all the hysteria, in the end it came down to the old question of "where's the money coming from?" And in the end, in came from the people of NSW through lotteries and higher taxes. These taxes surreptitiously were made more palatable **because they were spread over twice as many years** as was originally planned. **Not that anyone planned it this way.** Back in 1957, for Joe Cahill and others, **it was hold your breath and go. If you want a brave new world, someone has to be brave.**

MUSIC FOR THE SHARKS

The proposal by the Beach Broadcasting Company to play music to the beaches round the nation met with great hostility. This was a time when portable radios were all the rage, and when sonorous old jalopies without mufflers were making life hell for anyone who could hear. The idea that one of the few sanctuaries, the beach, could be desecrated brought forth lots of writers determined to fight on the beaches of Australia.

One early scribe was happy with the idea. He suggested that the music be played at double the acceptable volume, and directed equally out to sea. He was prepared to swim, even after a shark alarm, because he expected that properly chosen music would lull the sharks into tranquility.

He went on to speculate on what type of music would be best, and concluded that soft, smooth chamber music from strings might be best. Certainly, he said, raucous rock-and-roll would be dangerous, and at the other end, so too would be Beethoven and Tchaikovsky. He, wisely I thought, suggested that some trial and error would be necessary, and after a few hundred tragedies, we could expect to have enough data to make informed judgments.

Other writers weighed in with their wisdom. The Editor of the *SMH* pointed out that the promoters expected to have a **"captive audience of 200,000 prisoners" for their advertisements** on a good day. The Editor went on to say that an initiative such as this is difficult to stamp out once it gains a foothold, and that **now** is the time to protest.

He concluded with "the idea of radios blaring from every clubhouse spaced every 50 feet across our beaches is enough to horrify the most easy-going Australian amphibian."

Letter-writers joined in with condemnation.

Letters, Fred Wade. I read with dismay of the proposal to broadcast music on the beaches.

For five days our ears are blasted by a variety of noises – blaring radios being a prime offender. It is a blessed relief to escape to our beaches, to enjoy play of wind and wave, and the quiet sun.

The "music" mentioned would, doubtless, consist of horrible American crooners, and raucous dance bands. Spare us, then, this cacophonic din which would jangle the nerves and make the day hideous.

Letters, Norman Lloyd. Is there nowhere we can get away from the noise and blare of modern life? One simply cannot understand the necessity for being constantly assaulted by a barrage of sound wherever one goes. Is not this generation capable of living for even an hour or two without the noise of a radio or loudspeaker?

Letters, J R J Wilson. Your two sub-leaders have said all that should be said on this subject in far more temperate terms than the proposals deserve. All that needs to be done, as you remark, is for the public to demonstrate to their local councils that they are implacably opposed to vandalism of the kind proposed.

The best of music broadcast in these circumstances would be intolerable; to have to listen to the nauseating fatuities of advertisers, insupportable. Every council should assure the public that it will not, under any conditions, give permission for this nuisance to be created.

Comment. The idea of raising easy money for no effort appealed to some few of the lifesavers' movement. But the vast majority of them were as offended by the idea as were the general public. Local Councils, too, found the scheme odious, so the end result was that, in most places, no such scheme was adopted.

CHAPLAINS ON THE FACTORY FLOOR

Automation was a new word entering the English dictionary. It was obvious from US and British experience that the jobs of all sorts of workers were under threat because of the advent of machines that could do repetitive work cheaper than the current workforce. So workers here were startled by the new thought that they might **not have a job for life**, that they could be replaced by a machine, and their old skills would no longer be needed.

This applied to most parts of the workforce. Miners, wharfies, railway staff, clerks, and most jobs you could think of. All workers were conscious of this new threat. When they saw Time and Motion experts with their stopwatches out timing their every move, and when they were made to punch a fancy bundy on starting and finishing work, their hackles rose. When management talked about trailing new machinery, or actually introduced it, their reaction was to strike.

Put this against a background of the ongoing battle between management and the Communist-led unions, the industrial workers of this nation were confused, a bit scared for their future, and determined not to budge an inch.

Enter the Reverend Alan Walker. This much-respected clergyman was outspoken and often gave society a prod when it needed it. Recently, he had suggested that major industries make chaplains **available to workers in company time** to counsel them on larger social matters that were worrying them. Clearly, Walker and his supporters did not see this initiative as becoming a tool for management in controlling the workers. Rather, he saw it as providing guidance and perspective to troubled employees.

He was supported by the clergy generally, as you might expect. There were also other bodies that thought the idea had merits. This Letter below captures much of the spirit of Alan Walker.

Letters, H W Baker, Church of England, Parramatta.
Adequate preparation should ensure that all parties were sufficiently happy about it in advance. It is not new: it has been done elsewhere.

Christian opinion shares a broad objective in human relations in industry with all really thoughtful opinion. The worst outcome of the "industrial revolution" was the notion that **human beings** should be regarded not as personalities of infinite value, but **as mere units of production**, from top management down. Today it is realised that this notion is utterly out of date, but it lives on in practice, and it is not an easy matter to rethink all the details of practical arrangements in accord with a change of principle.

The principle can be arrived at from various points of view: an employee may feel he wishes to be regarded more as a human being, because he is one; modern management may see that treating employees as human personalities will improve production. But because the truth about people really is that we are all children of God and that the integrity of personality is sacred, that is the only basis on which mutual faith can develop, and these results be included in a greater result.

Informed Christian opinion has no thought of supplanting those in labour and management whose task it must be to work out the practical arrangements all the time. It is natural that they should wish to put the question: "Tell me in detail just what you propose" – but there isn't any detail to propose until the parties concerned in a particular place feel they wish to accept the principle, and meet to see how a works chaplaincy, as a very elementary step, could be set up among them.

The fear of a harassed union official or production manager that it would be only another complication is easily appreciated, but that is just what a works chaplain would take most pains to avoid.

It would be unfortunate if leaders of different sections in industry should condemn this excellent thought-provoking suggestion just on a quick reaction, and so further postpone the deliberate consideration it merits.

The Union movement was not so sanguine. There was an immediate response to Walker from the ACTU Secretary that unions do not interfere in religious matters and that religions should not interfere with union matters. After that, other more sensible arguments emerged. How impartial would the advice be? It might mean that the undoubtedly Christian advice of the chaplain would be in direct conflict with the Communist inspired union. For example, at the philosophical level, the Communists hated the bosses. Would the chaplain tell workers to love the bosses? Surely that would mean that they then become more compliant with company demands, and not stand shoulder-to-shoulder with the union.

At a more pragmatic level, management would soon be wanting to introduce some measure of automation. It would say that greater production was for the benefit of all. There was every chance that the chaplain would accept this as true, and convey it to worried workers. But the union would say that automation was for the sole purpose of cutting jobs. Whether or not this was true, you would then have the chaplain acting as the agent of management in giving advice. The unions were not happy with this.

Then there were more practical difficulties. Could the clergy find enough time to make a real dent? Would they be paid? **Surely the unions would demand that they would be.** In which case, they would be paid by management, and then become employees of the company. Could they then give impartial advice?

The arguments against the scheme mounted up, and in the end, I know of no company that adopted the plan. Some of the larger ones much later adopted the idea of a resident psychologist who could talk through issues with individuals. But that was a long way away from the idea of a religious chaplain.

THE ROLE OF THE UN

At the end of last year, the Suez and Hungarian crises stirred Australians out of their apathy towards overseas events. The newspapers were full of stories from those two nations, and the Letters to the Editors ran hot.

Sadly though, the UN had not met the challenge. It raised its hands in horror when the Brits were **talking** tough, then it raised them again when the Russians **acted** tough. But the Brits, and the French, and the Russians had the power of veto in the UN. So no action could be organised. In all, **the UN had followed the principle that might was right.**

Over the last six`months, nothing had changed. **Except that perceptions of its weakness grew stronger.** The pre-war League of Nations had crashed and burned after it failed to slow down Mussolini when he invaded Abyssinia in 1930.

Now it seemed that the UN might be headed for the same ineffectual fate as the League. Hopefully not, but it did not bounce back after the 1956 crises, and it seemed unlikely to do so.

GROWING TRADE CONCERNS

Britain was talking about joining with the states of Europe to form a common market. That would be a group of countries that traded with each other, and reduced tariffs between them. If this grand planning came to fruition, it would mean that Britain's close trading ties with Australia would be severed, and that we would need to find new export markets for our goods.

At the moment, the odds were that such a scheme would not get off the ground. Certainly it was not worrying the general population, though some Government Ministers were quite concerned. In any case, the politics of overseas trade will be raised again through the year, and we will leave further discussion of them to later chapters.

THE BOMB IS TO BLAME

The A-bombs on Japan were dropped 12 years ago, and the immediate tragedy of them had faded a bit. So that now, when things went wrong for people, someone said facetiously "Blame it on the bomb." This applied particularly to the weather. As floods and fire and droughts inevitably took their toll, the bombs were blamed as the cause.

Now this clever little Letter quietly mocked that approach.

Letters, G Wachman. Why has no one yet blamed the atom bomb for the prolonged spell of **fine** weather?

ACTIONS AGAINST CHICKENS

Letters, Barrister. Surely the Commissioner for Police, Mr C J Delaney, did not go far enough when he said that if anyone died because of a game of "chicken", the culprit would be liable to a manslaughter charge.

Actually the correct charge would be murder, which is defined by Section 18 of the Crimes Act to include acts done "with reckless indifference to human life," and this is clearly the case with the game of "chicken."

SP BETTING IN HOSPITALS

Letters, Nora Bourke. If SP betting could be made legal to finance the opera house, why could it not be made legal to finance the hospitals? Any person who has spent time in any of our hospitals knows how much money goes out for SP bets. Every person who comes into the wards is commissioned to take out money for bets.

Would it not be better for a stand to operate in the hospital grounds (for the benefit of the hospital) than to allow the money to enrich outsiders, who acquire wealth without paying taxes?

SANITARY WORKERS AND THE CLERGY

Letters, (Ald.) A Heynes. In reporting the General Assembly of the Presbyterian Church you quote a speaker, Mr Stanley Smith as saying: "At present sanitary carters are paid more than our ministers." This is ridiculous.

The **inference is that these men are either of poor intellect or in a low stratum of industry**, or both. I consider the statement in very bad taste, especially when it comes from an elder of the Church. Surely if Mr Smith wanted to draw a comparison to show the inadequate pay of the ministers he could have done it in a better manner, for instance, by a comparison with the teaching profession.

The facts are that the sanitary carters are doing a job of work which, to say the least, is most distasteful. It is enough that they are the butt of many jokes, which I am sure they take in good part, but when a statement is made in public such as that by Mr Smith I consider a reply is called for by any serious-minded citizen.

JUNE NEWS ITEMS

Sydney police announced that the city had established **a new record. 70 motor vehicles were stolen at the weekend**, and that beats all previous efforts. By Sunday, most had been recovered, but many were burnt out or damaged. Police are aware that **many of the cars are used for playing chicken**. Similar situations have also developed in **other States** where the proportion of hoons is no smaller than in NSW.

Comment. I love the idea of *chicken*. It gives our disaffected youth something to do in their spare time.

"Ham" radio operators were sending messages into the ether trying to contact a man in New Guinea with news of illness in his family. This serves as a reminder that **communications in remote areas without telegraph and phones, was difficult. What a long way it was then from the satellites and internet of today.**

A man was fined ten Pounds in the Adelaide Court for using **an electric razor to shave himself** while driving at 45 mph. **Texting was not yet listed as an offence.**

A Victorian poultry farmer, after losing hundreds of chooks to theft, had **fired a rifle at a running intruder**. He intended to coerce the runner to stop, or at most to injure him and allow his capture. **The shot however killed the intruder**….

The farmer was **initially sentenced to three years goal for manslaughter**, this was reduced to 18 months. He took the case all the way to the High Court, where his plea for dismissal was refused. Then as an act of clemency from the State, **he was released** on a good behaviour bond after 13 months....

This opens the question as to **what rights do farmers have to protect their property**. And leads to the same question for grocers and other persons with property. And finally, to **what rights do householders have**?

A woman in Portuguese East Africa has **given birth to quintuplets. Previously she had produced twins, then triplets, then quads.** All 14 of the children are living.

Well, I'll be blowed. The ALP State Conference did actually **approve the building of the Sydney Opera House**. The discussions were "long and protracted" and "bitter", and the decision proved that "Labor politicians are not just a bunch of hillbillies, without any artistic taste or aspirations." **No decision was made on financing the construction**.

Two hundred coal miners at the Northern NSW coal mine at Aberdare **decided to stage a sit-in strike** over sackings in the coal industry. They say they will remain underground until the NSW Premier promises some relief from redundancies. **A supply line sent in 360 meat pies for the men.** Some refused the pies because it was Friday, so battered fish and chips were also sent....

From tomorrow, **three hot meals a day** will be provided by the Women's Auxiliary. Magazines, packs of playing cards, and darts and boards were sent underground. Colliery management said that **at this stage it would not cut off the supply of electricity to the men.**

RADIATION EFFECTS OF NUCLEAR BOMBS

As the world pondered the effects of the dropping of the bomb, various theories emerged about the **radiation** effects. These included that, given that we were at all times subject to some level of natural radiation, the incremental increase in dosage would be of no consequence to us.

At the other end of the spectrum, there were those who said that the increase was enough to affect our genes, and that many of us would die from radiation illnesses, and that future generations would be deformed and mutated.

Every time an atomic power exploded a new nuclear device, controversy over radiation flared up again. Some proponents gleefully pointed to the fact that people were not falling like flies, and that healthy babies were booming all round the world. Others said that ultimately the camel's back would break, and that maybe this latest test would prove to be the last straw.

Part of the problem was that the man in the street had no real knowledge of the processes involved. He had to rely on experts coming from universities and other powerful institutions. The trouble was that these learned people had vastly different views based on whatever set of so-called facts they looked at. Some of them too were **undoubtedly influenced by their own vested interests, such as job prospects**, and the desire for publicity. So that, in all, the average person had little real information to go on, and voiced his opinions with all the certainty goes hand in hand with true ignorance.

The Editor of the *SMH* had this to say: "Nothing is more maddening than the continued inability of eminent scientists to make up their minds about the dangers of atomic tests." He gave many examples of how Australian scientists disagree with each other. He ended with a plea for them to purge themselves of those political, emotional and moral prejudices that they are prey to just as much as ordinary citizens.

He had plenty of support from readers. And plenty from readers who were not so sure.

Letters, (Dr.) Colin S Gum. It is highly desirable that various eminent scientists, holding conflicting views, should express them individually in the Press. The fact that there are widespread disagreements between the experts is the simplest argument for concluding that no one has a really unbiased answer to the problem.

Because of the recent successes of scientific research applied to technological development, there has been a tendency by the public to regard the scientist as an infallible oracle. This view ignores the fact that science is, in a sense, a voyage of discovery, and that the frontiers of knowledge are only pieced together gradually. In the process of fitting the pieces together, a scientist is very lucky if he never makes a false statement here and there.

Present widespread disagreements between specialists indicate that, as yet, there is not sufficient scientific evidence available on which to decide on the nature of the radio-active risks of tests. Hence any decision on bomb-testing made by a scientist, or by any other person, is **basically a moral decision**.

An issue was raised by some writers that said any decisions on the effects of bombs must at this time be based not on scientific facts, but on emotion, politics, and pre-conceived bias. As if to prove this, the following Letter is offered.

Letters, C A F Court. The basic "human" instinct which **makes a man prefer survival to all else is an animal one and not worthy of human nature.** The free world rivals the Communist world not only in power but also in ideals. We strive, I do not say with complete success, to guarantee certain rights to all human beings, and to achieve a government which mirrors as closely as possible the desires of the governed. That these ideals are influential is evidenced by the abundant lip-service paid to them by the Communists.

However, in the event of a Communist victory, not only the actuality of human rights and representative government but the very concept of them, would vanish from this planet. Men would sink into a sub-human existence of drabness, relieved by frightfulness, the life and welfare of each depending on a ponderous bureaucracy backed by a merciless "secret" police.

Faced with this prospect, people who love the human race just as much as Mrs Senior have made the agonising choice to continue nuclear weapon tests with the risks they may incur.

X-RAYS AND RADIATION

All of the above became more immediate when the Federal Government started to talk about **removing its backing for enforcing compulsory X-rays of the population.** The idea here was that TB was a dreadful disease, and that its treatment should begin with proper and early diagnosis. The Feds a few years ago launched an initiative, working with the States, to make most of the population undertake a regular X-ray of their chest to seek signs of the disease.

To achieve this, specially equipped vans were sent to various regions round the nation, and all eligible persons in that area were called upon to have an X-ray. It was compulsory to do so, and a fine would be levied for non-compliance.

Now, with all the talk about the effects of radiation, the question being asked was whether the radiation from these X-rays would be harmful. Would it be the extra radiation from this life-saving equipment that would be too much?

Letters, Athena Kenney. In view of the recent publicity given to the adverse effects of radiation, I wish to protest against the compulsory X-ray survey carried out by the Anti TB Association.

This X-ray examination may be excellent in many cases, but to be compelled, with the threat of a fine, to undergo such is a violation of human rights.

If a person of average good health is prepared to submit a certificate from his local doctor that his lungs appear to be in a sound condition, there should be no compulsory X-ray examination, if that person does not wish to be subjugated to such a test.

After all, this is supposed to be a free country. The poliomyelitis vaccine is not compulsory. Why then should the TB X-ray be compulsory? Why must we be compelled to submit our bodies to an examination we may not wish to have?

It may be argued that the small amount of radiation from the TB X-ray is harmless. This would not be so when one is subjected to a number of X-rays, and who can tell to what extent each and every one of us may be exposed in the future to radiation.

The case could be that a perfectly healthy person may submit to the compulsory X-ray. Then some drastic accident or sickness could befall him, making it essential for him to be X-rayed perhaps once, perhaps many times. Would it not be better then, that the TB X-ray had been omitted? That unnecessary X-ray may be the final clincher.

Letters, MD. Arguing against compulsory X-rays, A Kenney says that, if a person is prepared to submit a certificate from his local doctor that his lungs "appear to be in sound condition," no compulsory examination should be necessary.

As one of the medical practitioners your writer speaks about, I would like her to know that not one GP in a thousand would be prepared to issue such a certificate unless the examination included a chest X-ray.

As to her contention that a compulsory X-ray is "a violation of human rights," I would say that so also is the indiscriminate spreading of TB. Compulsory X-rays are not meant as a weapon against the population as a whole. The majority of people have enough good sense to have X-rays without being forced. Unfortunately, however, there is a minority group which cannot be persuaded by normal methods. Only compulsion will work in their case.

As far as Miss Kenney's fear of adverse radiation is concerned, two authoritative Australian bodies as recently as last month issued reports which put the situation in its proper perspective. They said that the danger is minuscule, and fear of them was not rational.

Letters, A G. Although I can understand Athena Kenney's concern about TB X-rays as a possible radiation danger, I wonder how she would react if, like me, she met with a case of TB in her own family which would have been found too late if an X-ray had not been taken when it was?

My 18-year-old boy went to a doctor for a physical check-up about three years ago, was tested in the usual way with a stethoscope, and was told he was perfectly all right.

Two months later, by a sheer fluke, he was X-rayed by one of those mobile vans which happened to be visiting his place of employment. When the X-ray was examined, he was told he was suffering from TB and had been so for at least a year! He is now back to health, thanks to the people who took his X-ray.

Letters, A E Hancock. Many angles have been discussed through your columns in the current X-ray controversy.

I would suggest that people subject to radiation for therapy, extensive investigations and even shoe fittings, etc., should be issued with cards whereby the date and duration of radiation could be recorded.

At present, it is possible for a person to be subjected to X-rays from several sources, without the respective medical authorities being aware of their full x-ray history.

Letters, Leslie S Andrews. Is it not a fact that too much compulsion steals away from man that very quality which has made him pre-eminent?

I refer to that quality of reason without which man is the victim of fear, uncertainty and disease.

One writer said that if everything thought to be for the good of the community could be forced onto the general public, then life would not be worth living. He went on to say that most Australians reach adolescence without having been exposed to TB. **Therefore they are open to any infection they meet.** They can however be immunised, giving 80 per cent protection. He claims that a vaccine has been used on natives in New Guinea with success, and that it had also been used in the Scandinavian countries for years. Prevention, he concluded, is better than cure.

Comment. Mind you, good though his advice might be, he has strayed a long way from the question of whether even X-rays of the foot might be critically harmful.

In any case, the Government soon after dropped the compulsion, as the incidence of TB fell with better food and housing and sanitation, and with more effective methods of isolating the disease. And a bit later, with the widespread use of vaccines and tests.

ARE RUSSIANS MISERABLE BAD GUYS?

Prior to the WWII, according to our newspapers and our governments, the Russians were bad guys and everything they did or thought was terrible. During WWII, they decided after a while to fight Hitler, and so they suddenly became good guys. But after the war, when they went their own Communist way, they were on the nose again.

Thus, their actions were all bad, their political system was dictatorial and coercive, and their people were intimidated, they were universally impoverished, and they were miserable. So wholeheartedly had this picture been promulgated in Australia that it was taken for granted that it was a true picture of a nation that almost no Australian had ever visited.

The Letter below paints another picture. It is so very different from the one usually presented that it must have generated a lot of discussion in the *SMH* editorial office before they decided to publish it.

Letters, I A Rush. I should like a support the view expressed by your correspondent, Mrs M Senior, that approval on continuing atom tests is an emotion corrupted by accepted current opinions.

After living and working in Moscow for 12 years prior to and during World War II, I cannot agree **that universal extinction might be preferable to life as lived behind the "Iron Curtain."**

In fact, in Moscow, and on holiday in various villages far and wide in the country, I found people reasonably cheerful and enjoying life, just as here. For young folk in particular, with all doors of education thrown wide open to them, and fewer weary hours spent in queues (mum or granny did this), life was bright.

The police State existed, and during the terror years of 1937 and 1938 was responsible for the death and arrest of far more people than were killed and maimed by cars in the USA, for instance, during the same years. But on the average, I should say, cars kill and maim **far more people** in highly motorised countries than the political police do in Communist countries, and the victims are more indiscriminately struck down. Yet we do not go about trembling in fear; nor do they.

The police State in Russia is more truly understood as a **continuation of Russian historical tradition** than as a unique contribution of Communism. National traditions change and mellow, and there is every appearance that this process is taking place in the USSR today. **Our own hostility and militarism is one of the factors retarding the change.**

Your correspondent, C A F Court, and others, are terrorised by a bogy largely of their own making. If they would only spend a few months living under the system they fear, its undeniable faults would shrink into just proportion, many attractive features would become apparent, and they would laugh at the near-schizophrenic state into which they had previously allowed themselves to be drawn.

The response was immediate and predictable. There were quite a few people who had different points of view, and I give two below.

Letters, Philip F Crowley. I agree with Mr Rush that universal extinction would not be better than life behind the Iron Curtain. But I object strongly to the implied reference that, even if cessation of atomic tests meant the acceptance of "enlightened leadership," this state would be reasonably attractive.

Mr Rush's comparison of USSR liquidation figures and USA road toll deaths makes me wonder if Mr Rush considers people as statistics or as persons. Certainly cars are sometimes indiscriminate in their choice of victims, but when they claim a victim in the privacy of his own home at 3 o'clock in the morning, then it is headline news.

The statements that "all doors of education are thrown wide open" to youth and that the police State is mellowing are flatly contradicted by the Supreme Presidium itself. In fact, many sincere Communists are disillusioned by the fact that the police State, far from "withering away" in its idyllic state (as postulated by Marx, Lenin, and Stalin), is, in fact, developing a healthier appetite all the time.

Finally, Mr Rush says that we would laugh at our fears if we were only to sample for some months a taste of this unique dictatorship. Did the people of Hungary laugh their heads off or did they have them knocked off, not by automobiles but by tanks?

Letters, Hungarian Refugee. I was deeply astonished by reading the letter of I A Rush on the "attractive features" of Russian life.

I have not lived in Russia, but I lived in Hungary up to the end of 1956. Ten years ago, I witnessed how the small Communist Party, led by Moscow, took power over the overwhelming majority of anti-communist Hungarians. Mr Rush says the common people in Russia "do not go about trembling in fear." Well, Hungarians did for the last 10 years, and presumably do so now too. Their reward was a steadily decreasing standard of living, a shortage of food in a country which was formerly a large exporter of agricultural products, and a deteriorated quality of goods produced by the socialised industry.

Mr Rush says that "for young folk ... life was bright." But in Hungary these young folk, brought up by the Communists, revolted against the Russian and had to be killed by thousands, in order to be taught how "bright" their life was under Russian rule.

Please do not put my name under this letter, I have relatives in Hungary.

These emotional arguments brought their own response.

Letters, T Brooks. Your correspondents pointed out that Russia was ruthless in putting down the recent revolution in Hungary. In fact, the revolution was violent and a serious threat to the sovereignity of Russia. Whether you agree with Russia's presence in Hungary, surely you must agree that there is no other way to stop a revolution promoted by the wildest fanatics.

The important issue at the moment is living conditions in Russia, and how oppressive is the current regime to the ordinary citizen? I have no barrow to push, but from many years of constant visiting the country, I say that they are as happy as you and I are.

The two Letters you published do not address this matter, and simply try to **turn criticism of Russia's foreign policy into an attack on Russia in general.** This is hard to take from people who have never been near the country.

JULY NEWS ITEMS

Press report, July 1st. **The strike by underground miners** at Aberdare West Colliery entered its fourth day. **260 miners are still underground**, and strict sanitary rules have been introduced. Morale is high, and they have come together for **community singing** and performances by two solo artists. Food is being provided by pit-head volunteers....

July 2nd. The men were underground for 84 hours, and then **the strike was over.** The NSW Premier said that three weeks work would be provided for the miners removing coal stored "at grass". Also, that talks would be held to find jobs for the dismissed men....

In reality, **these concessions were not worth much**. But they did let the Miners Federation retreat from the strike **with the face-saving claim of victory**.

Don't rock the boat. Remember the official from the NSW Taxpayers Association who advocated that taxpayers should **claim a deduction for fares paid in getting to work**. Remember too that the Taxation Department was very firm **that deductions would not be allowed**....

This same gentleman, Mr Sindel, **was fired from his position** as honorary President of the Association. The committee did not agree with his advice, and dismissed him. They said that **his action interfered with the harmonious relations that currently existed between themselves and the Department**. So, that's why such deductions are still not allowed.

Australia and Japan signed a Trade Pact in July, and this was the first since WWII. The war ended 12 years ago, and since then **high tariffs and quotas have kept Japanese goods from our markets**. Part of the deal is that we in turn will sell more goods to Japan....

Large elements of the Australian public still hate the Japanese for their invasion and war-time atrocities. This deal will not find much favour with them.

July 8th. **Lew Hoad**, tennis champion in every sense of the word**, had just won the men's Wimbledon tournament, and decided to turn pro**. This meant that he will join American Jack Kramer's **circus of tennis professional** that is currently staging matches round the world....

Pros and amateurs are not allowed to play against each other. Hoad will join the same traveling troupe that his "twin", Ken Rosewall, joined a few years ago.

Be careful. The Asian flu is starting to claim victims. At the moment, **the epidemic is in its infancy**, and it's just like the normal flu. But over a few years, it will spread across the world, and kill many of the vulnerable.

Be doubly careful. Sightings of flying saucers are on the increase. A typical example was seen in the NSW town of Katoomba on July 19th. Bright lights, perhaps with boosting rockets, **the vision lasted about six minutes and was seen by dozens of sober folk.** So far, there have been no claims that anyone was kidnapped and taken away as specimens for study. But, **such claims were no rarity overseas.**

THE ADVENT OF BILLY GRAHAM

Billy Graham was a Southern Baptist minister who was making a name for himself as an evangelist stumping round the US and elsewhere, trying to convert the middle class to his form of Christianity. His message was love of God and thy neighbour, avoid obvious traps, be charitable and law abiding. This was the same as the gospel preached in Christian churches right across the world. His difference was that **he used American show-business tactics to reach vast audiences**, and he preached with such a fervour and immediacy that he roused listeners from their Sunday lethargy, often to a state of near-hysterical engagement with the word of God.

The Christianity he taught was straight from the least obscure areas of the Bible. Nothing complicated like theology, no mention of the history of religion or of Church Fathers or Creeds. His mission was to **sell Sunday School Christianity to a mass market**, and to move languid listeners towards active evangelism for **a Bible-driven Christianity**.

Graham had been successful across America for a few years and had recently returned triumphant from Britain. Now, he had set his sights on Australia, and several Protestant Churches here were joining together to make preparations for his visit. It was early days as yet, and his actual arrival turned out to be 18 months away.

Still, there was lots of preparation to do. **When he did start to preach in Australia**, he held a dozen rallies at the biggest venues in this nation, like the Sydney Showground. They were attended by tens of thousands of people from a broad range of society. He was promoted by thousands of volunteers who set up stalls in High Streets across the eastern seaboard, pressuring and inducing strangers to come to the rallies. The rallies were blessed by the well-trained singing of mass choirs backed by tasteful Southern music. Graham was able to work up his audience to a near-frenzy of enthusiasm, so that hundreds of attendees readily came to the front and attested their devotion to God and his divine works. **In all, it was great show-business, and certainly did no harm.**

The question being raised even at this early stage was whether it would do any good. Would the effects wear off quickly, would church attendances increase and then hold the increase, would society in general benefit in any material or spiritual way from Graham's visit? There were quite diverse opinions on this.

A Reverend from Victoria was not keen on the visit.

Letters, (Rev) W F Hart. We have had here in Australia, in recent years, many of these itinerant evangelists, and a great deal of money has been spent on the rent of halls and publicity, and approximately 1p.c. of the population has attended each "mission."

In London, Graham filled the Harringay arena almost every night for two months, with a total attendance of over 800,000 people, and another 50,000 at a meeting in Hyde Park, but these figures are not impressive when you dissect them, for then you discover that 15 p.c. of the attendances were of children under 11 years of age, and 67 p.c. were children under 14.

Obviously any decisions made by these children that they were going to become followers of Christ are of very little value or significance; particularly with those whose parents are not themselves regular churchgoers.

Children who have to get themselves dressed and get their own breakfast on Sunday mornings in order to go to church and Sunday school while their parents stay in bed, invariably find their enthusiasm and interest gone within a few weeks.

The people who have to be converted are not the children, but their fathers, and men above 30 years of age were conspicuously absent from Graham's gatherings both in England and America.

The churches here in Australia need a great influx of men into them, but the naïve, fundamentalist preaching of Mr Billy Graham proves to be pathetically inept and unable to help men, and it will be a pity if we waste our time and money in Australia on the type of evangelistic campaign that has already proved unsuccessful overseas.

This Letter brought some quick responses. Some writers are a bit hard to follow, but in any case I suggest you read them just to see how much heat this subject had already generated.

Letters, (Rev. Dr) E H Watson, General Secretary, Baptist Union of NSW. There are many in this city who will strongly disagree with the Rev W F Hart in his statements regarding Dr Billy Graham. For Mr Hart to state that the "naïve fundamentalist preaching of Mr Billy Graham proves to be pathetically inept and unable to help men" is not true to the facts of the case. Such a statement is both incorrect and damaging.

A number of the leading British newspapers heartily commend him. Many free church leaders spoke of the impact of his ministry upon the church life of England. Mr Hart discounts decisions made by young people. Perhaps he has the answer for the present juvenile delinquency problem and is not concerned with the fact that in 1962 there will be half as many 15-year-olds as there were in 1956. Some of us in middle life can testify to the value of decisions made in childhood.

The most interesting dissection is that of decisions made during Dr Graham's Harringay campaign. The largest age group was that of 12-18 years and the second largest 19-29 years.

May God send Dr Billy Graham to Australia!

Letters, R G Davidson, Superintendent Minister, Glebe Methodist Mission. For years now, some of us have been trying to convince our hearers that effective evangelism for this generation must have a sense of responsibility toward man's total needs. That means the message of the evangelist must be organically related to science, education, industry, and politics.

In his "Mission to the Nation" addresses, the Rev Alan Walker made some headway along this path. With the coming of Dr Billy Graham, I, for one, believe that much ground will be lost, for Dr Graham's evangelism is, albeit unwittingly, none the less irresponsible.

It is profoundly disconcerting to find how many people on the fringe of the Church think of us as taking part in a kind of harmless racket – kidding ourselves along with impossible dogmas and bearing amiable false witness in the interests of an anaemic ethic.

In particular, Dr Graham's use of the slogan "The Bible says" is irresponsible.

As with the Greek classics, the Bible can be made to say almost anything you want it to say, according to the place at which you decide to open it.

I am not here attempting to evaluate the Bible, I am anxious to bring home to the conscience of the reader that an evangelist who uses the Bible as a bludgeon stands condemned before the honest of his Lord.

The Nemesis that will follow the coming of Dr Graham is that once more the church has indulged in a feast of fervent irresponsibility, and so loses, for a still greater time, creditability among those whom it seeks most earnestly to influence.

A few of the real heavies had their say.

Letters, D W B Robinson, Senior Lecturer, Moore Theological College. For a Christian to regard Dr Graham's use of the phrase, "The Bible says," as irresponsible is astonishing, since Jesus Himself repeatedly used an identical phrase, "It is written," when quoting Scripture (Matthew 4).

Of course, the devil is reported to have done the same: which means that those who quote the Bible in this way should take care to quote it properly. But to charge Dr Graham with irresponsibility in this matter, without any supporting evidence of a misuse of Scripture, is surely itself an irresponsible criticism.

Letters, Douglas J Golding, Chatswood South Methodist Church. Dr Davidson's complaint against Billy Graham appears to be that he preaches from the Bible, which, he claims, "can be made to say almost anything you want it to say." No doubt it can, but only if its statements are taken out of context, or its message "edited" to conform to some preconceived prejudice or ideal.

But Billy Graham aims always to preach Bible truth pure and undefiled, which is the foundation of Christianity. Part at least of his success is due to his candour and honesty in restoring to the modern world both the message and the ardour of the first apostles.

Dr Davidson's remarks are unfortunately typical of the creed of a number of ministers, not only in the Methodist denomination, who have permitted their undoubted intellectual power and their university doctorates to destroy essential Christian humility.

The clerical correspondence continued for two weeks. One spokesman for the Seventh Day Adventists said that a return to the simple Bible, a la Billy Graham, was needed to prevent our land falling into a form of neo-paganism. He finished with the earnest prayer that "God bless Billy Graham and to all who make the Bible foremost."

Another writer pulled out some statistics from a crusade in Boston. These purported to show that the crusade had been of no lasting benefit. He ended with the challenging summation that any campaign "would not bring peace or decrease human strife, because it represents mainly a cheap self-gratification for the psycho-neurotics and sham-religious persons."

Comment.   You can see some real venom among these writers, all of them clergymen. This clash of minds went on and on, and in the end was closed by the Editor.

The end result was that no one changed their minds, no one saw any utility in a counter argument, and the clerical community remained divided, and indeed in some cases, bitterly divided.

The humble churchgoers were more emphatic. By the time Graham **left** here, he had preached to over a million persons, he claimed. Months and years later, attempts were made to evaluate the permanent effects of his crusade, and the results were mixed, to say the least.

THE BRAVE WORLD OF SPORTS PROS

When the war ended and Australia resumed cricket Test matches against England, it came as a surprise to many that the old pre-war distinctions between amateurs and professionals still existed in English cricket. It was noticeable here when the 1946 MCC team came to Australia. The few pros among the Poms had their own dressing room and their own entrance to the playing field, and there was a noticeable difference in their attitudes. We in Australia were still all amateurs in cricket, so we had no similar barriers.

Tennis world-wide was still generally lily white up till about 1950. Then Jack Kramer, a former American Davis Cup player, started to form a troupe of about eight professionals who toured the world playing each other, and receiving additional bonuses each time they won. By 1957, this "circus" was well established on the tennis scene, but it was not at all acceptable to the stalwarts of amateur tennis.

Amateur tennis continued on as if the pros did not exist. The Australian Open, and events in France, and the USA and also Wimbledon were the big fixtures, with a myriad of lesser supporting events on the calendar. Amateurs were not allowed to play in pro events, nor in so-called **open** events. Nor could there be any joint practice. Any form of reconciliation or compromise was made difficult because the officials from both sides were scarcely speaking together.

By the time Hoad won Wimbledon in 1957, the two camps were miles apart. Kramer had already poached Australian champions Sedgman and McGregor, and more recently

Rosewall. Now Hoad turned pro. It looked like amateur tennis was becoming just a breeding ground for pro tennis, and that as soon as an amateur matured enough, he would give up his amateur status for the fortunes of pro tennis.

So, Hoad's decision re-opened this can of worms.

Letters, William Burnett. It is high time a larger question than the defection of amateurs to professionalism in tennis is faced. Why should not the major international contests be made "open" events?

The line of demarcation between amateurism and professionalism in lawn tennis today is noticeably thin; it should be declared "non est". Then lawn tennis all over the world will have the best of both worlds.

Letters, G T Perkins. The other regrettable aspect of the situation is the spectacle of yet another of our tennis champions forsaking the amateur ranks to make a fortune out of what was once only intended to be a game. The Hoads' contention that they need that amount of money to make themselves and their child financially secure for the future is too absurd for me to comment without being rude.

Finally, the point has now been reached, as a result of the example of so many of our leading post-war players, when the following question can well be posed: Has competitive tennis been allowed by its devotees in Australia to become merely the ladder whereby they can climb to the pinnacle of fame and then turn the sport into a money-making concern, and amass a fortune?

These perfectly reasonable Letters were followed the same day by a comment from Sir Norman Brookes, the voice of the Lawn Tennis movement in Australia. He concluded with **"Disgusting. Hoad couldn't have done this in a shabbier way."** The *SMH* laid in the boot as well. The Editor railed against him because "he can hardly be considered a shining exemplar of good manners", and added that "morally he cuts a very poor figure."

What had Hoad done to get these powerful figures off-side? A few days earlier he had won the most prestigious tournament in the world of tennis. He was hailed as a national hero, kids everywhere worshiped him. The newspapers sold millions of copies on his victory. Now, he was being scourged in the Press. Why?

The answer was that he had joined the enemy. He was the **last of the real champions** that Australia currently had, and his defection left Australian tennis without that draw-card that Brookes and the *SMH* needed. Also, from Brookes' view, it appeared that the fight between amateur and pro tennis might now be drawn to a head, and it was certain that when that happened, purely amateur tennis would be the loser.

So, they gave Hoad a hard time. They claimed he had violated a contract with the Lawn Tennis Association. **In fact, he had not.** He had paid his way out in the manner required in his contract. They said he claimed right up till Wimbledon that he would not turn pro. Then he had signed with the enemy. This was a very naïve criticism, knowing full well from their own experiences how business is conducted and contracts are bargained.

These criticisms spilled over somewhat into the Letters column. This one below is hard to beat.

Letters, H R Hunt. I congratulate you on your leader with reference to Lewis Hoad. You have expressed to perfection the views of the vast majority of the public, who love tennis for the game itself.

I have noted the names of those of my acquaintances who have expressed approval of the manner in which Hoad has turned professional.

In any business transactions I may have with them, I will require, not only their word of honour, their written agreement signed, sealed and delivered, but in addition very ample security.

Comment. Tennis, as you know, is now "open" at the top level. The churlish attempts at the time of Hoad to denigrate his move were to no avail, as indeed they have been ineffective in other sports. Take for example, Rugby Union. It held out for decades, and now our older champions profitably fly to France for their last few playing years. Look at cricket. Once a player rises to State level, he gets an agent, and then he starts to wonder how much cash he can get from the game.

Some of us old-timers might have a few nostalgic pangs now and then about **the characters** of old world sport, but there's nothing wrong with the new set-up as I see it. Certainly, the athletic prowess of the youngsters of today far exceeds that of the old world, and that has to be a good thing for the sport and spectators.

SELL-OUT TO AMERICA

US influence in Australia had been big and growing since the war, and right now you could find it everywhere. It had recently been given quite a fillip from the Suez crisis at the end of 1956, when the Brits had behaved very badly and had weakened their influence round the world. There were many in Australia who were getting more conscious **that it was with America, not with Britain, that our future lay**.

You could see it everywhere. In clothing, movies, hit songs, hot dogs, baseball caps, to name a silly few. More significantly, our defences, our military, our balance of trade, all showed us pointing to the east and not the west.

Some people were talking some delightfully foolish stuff. One Letter writer suggested that we could become a State of America if the USA would give every man, woman, and child one million dollars each to spend as we chose.

A *SMH* editorial suggested that we should do more with our Australia Day celebrations. It extolled the activities on big days in the US, and suggested all the bally-hoo of parades and civil ceremonies were something that we should follow.

But among our own level heads, there was this writer who had his own idea on what constituted a better way of celebrating our National Day.

Letters, Brian J O'Brien. Your leader page of July 13 was devoted substantially to a detailed account of the plans of various public bodies to transform the celebration of January 26, the Australian national day. I read the article with interest but failed to discover any given reason for the transformation other than the smallness of the Australian celebrations when compared with the American activities of July 4.

If there is a desire for "miles of flags," for radio stations to broadcast only Australian works, again this is a matter for free choice.

But if officialdom tries to get me to raise my voice and shout in public displays of joy because of the actions of other officials of long ago, then I will disappoint you. It was not the first landing which was important of itself, but rather what has happened and is happening since.

If I wish, I shall remember in my own quiet way. But in general, I shall celebrate the "holiday" in my usual manner – I shall have a nice quiet rest, away from officialdom and crowds of noisy people. And I feel it would be better for those crowds (and for Australia) if they stayed home and thought rather than entered the streets and shouted.

NEWS AND VIEWS

The Opera House again. The NSW government has decided that the Opera House will be **paid for by appeals to the public** for funds. Maybe they will run special lotteries. **But not from any form of taxes. Good luck!!**

The Doll struck the jackpot. Ray Lawler's *Summer of the Seventeenth Doll,* still performing in London, had landed a **Hollywood contract to be made into a film**. Lawler himself will gain **a meagre 80,000 Pounds** from the sale of rights.

A bushfire destroyed a dozen properties near the NSW regional city of Lismore. A local **newspaper** asked "does it make sense for people to **let trees and shrubs and wheat stubble come up on to their land**? Sometimes, right up to their back door?..."

Question. **Year after year, such fires**, many of them much bigger, **kill people and destroy homes** right round Australia. **The same Paper** asked "**Does it make any more sense now than it did 60 years ago?**"

AUGUST NEWS ITEMS

A number of children have **climbed into refrigerators** and the door has been locked. Once inside, the **child has no way of releasing the door**, and a dozen children have been killed or badly damaged nationwide as a result. Most States are **making it compulsory** for dumpers of fridges, at public Council tips, **to remove the doors first**.

At the BHP site of Newcastle, **engineers moved a huge chimney stack, 230 feet high and 11 feet across, a distance of fifty feet**, without cracking a brick....

They removed a few layers of bricks from the base, and replaced them periodically with jacks. Then, with a combination of jacks and railway tracks and restraining ropes, they moved the stack, still vertical into its new position. Then it was bolted down. **Comment. Wow!**

The game of chicken has been spreading quickly. A driver of a diesel rail car reported **that two three-year-old children** stood on the track facing him, and when he slowed down almost to a stop**, they jumped clear shouting "chicken".**

Comment. It makes me happy to see American culture being so readily accepted by our littlies.

August 7th. **The fund-raising for the Opera House** opened officially. At a function at the Sydney Town Hall, the NSW Premier read out a list of founding donors that included major companies and personalities. Contributions were accepted from the public, and a swarm of clerks was kept busy issuing receipts to small cash donors....

The total donated at the end of one hour was 235 thousand Pounds. The total cost is estimated at 3.5 million Pounds....

A further 295 Pounds was **raised** among celebrities back-stage after the ceremony as those assembled **paid to give and receive kisses from and to each other**. The lucky ones included singer Joan Hammond, Lord Mayor Harry Jensen, designer Joern Utzon, and ABC's Charles Moses.

The Labor Party is still being torn apart by internal fighting. The Labor Premier in **Queensland** has just been sacked. Several **Federal** MPs are calling for the resignation of Labor leader, Doc Evatt. Factions are attempting to oust **NSW** Premier Cahill. All this is generating bad headlines for the Labor Party. **More and more people are saying that Labor will never regain power in Federal politics while Evatt remains leader.**

Trams will be replaced by buses in the main streets of Sydney in December. Other major cities are reducing tram numbers at the same time...

In Sydney, people were horrified by front-page photographs of **retired trams being burnt**. Authorities said that **they tried to sell them**, but if they could not, they were burned. Many people thought this was a waste and suggested that **efforts to sell them were scarcely visible to the public.**

NO-NAME GAMBLING

Many Australians like to gamble. No matter how much anyone sermonises at them, or logically points out the folly of doing so, these people will bet on something. But there was not much scope for them to do so legally. There was no TAB, betting on the horses and dogs was restricted to the racetrack, casinos were only now available in a few States and only to people who could travel to them.

In many States, at various times, raffles had to be licensed by State governments, and housie-housie could not pay out cash prizes. Poker machines at the time were mere playthings, with fruit machines still the most common form. Even where the modern one-armed bandits were in use, they were three wheelers, often restricted to one shilling a play, and florin machines were rare in the country. Many clubs insisted that a one-penny machine was available, and indeed some said that one machine could be played with no coins at all. In all, adult serious betting was well and truly forced underground.

So law-abiding citizens by the millions used SP bookies to bet on horses, and half a million more found their way to gambling premises where they could play two-up or baccarat. These premises could be in swish city units, or in tin sheds at the back of beyond. They were raided regularly by the police, and those present paid a fine, and normally returned next night to a different place. Some of the bigger schools floated from one venue to another at midnight to foil the cops. One well-reported raid last year took place in a large Sydney cemetery, with about 40 men and women arrested after dramatic chases through the tombstones.

The proceedings at the gambling dives were well established. The police would come, take the name and address of players, and see them off the premises. Next day, charges would be laid in Court, and a fine would be imposed.

By 1957, all of this had developed over time into a charade. **The fines were now paid by the gambling establishment**, so the punters were not out of pocket. Then, in court they were **represented by a single solicitor paid for by the same establishment**. On top of this, the punters by now had learned to **give false names and addresses to the police**. Any name would do. Just make up one, or use the name of someone you disliked.

Of course, this was made possible because **the police had no way of checking names and addresses**. The only possible means of identification in those days was a driver's licence. But you would be surprised at how many affluent-looking gamblers had no cars and thus no driving licence. So, police had no way of checking and, by now, had given up trying.

The whole point of the police raids **had degenerated into revenue raising exercises.** The police chiefs and leading government officials assured the public, with their hands on their hearts, that they were trying to stamp out gambling, but this was just another part of the charade.

This came to a head in 1957 at the NSW regional city of Penrith. Locals there were protesting loudly at the system, and their cries were making it into the national Press. But they were a perverse lot. Their complaint was not that about the folly of the police efforts to stamp out gambling, but rather that the money from the fines was being **diverted from local purposes to the coffers of the State. Local money was going to finance developments in Sydney.**

The State big-wigs made all the usual noises. There was a lot of talk about "perfidiousness of gambling", and "moral responsibility", and "perspicacity". There were promises that "local equity" would be preserved in future, and that "gambling would be stamped out, for the benefit of the community." But these were idle words of course, and the system easily withstood this storm in a tea-cup.

Comment. Such was the gambling scene **right around Australia**. A harsh repressive scene held in place by governments determined to get as much money, from easy targets, as they could. All in the name of promoting a virtuous State.

Less than a decade later, when the TABs were created in all States, millions were free to place bets, and did so with relish. The gambling dens in sleazy premises have almost disappeared, and incidentally the revenue to the States increased beyond belief. Granted, there are still problems for the perpetual loser. But for most, it is **what you might describe as a win-win situation.**

IT SIMPLY IS NOT DONE.

In Britain, Lord Altrincham was a former officer of the Brigade of the Guards, and was educated at Eton and Oxford. Despite this pedigree, **he described the Queen's speaking as "a pain in the neck"**, and that her "utterances were those of a priggish schoolgirl", and that if she wanted a truly classless society, she should get rid of her "present entourage of people of the tweedy sort."

Various members of the aristocracy thought otherwise. One said the commentary was "absolutely disgusting and completely untrue." Another said the author **should be shot. Or hounded out of the country.** There were a number of *"highly objectionables"* and *"impertinents."*

The *Manchester Guardian* **summed up the mood in Britain with "any criticism of the Royal Family is a sacrilege." Lord Altrincham was a bit contrite.** He responded with "All I meant to do was point out that Her Majesty had a good opportunity to benefit many, and that her words did not seem to be doing that."

In Australia, friends of the monarch spoke out. The first two Letters are vaguely supportive of the criticism.

Letters, J Webster. The critics of Lord Altrincham seem in their zeal to have misread what he really did say. The only personal strictures were on her Majesty's voice and delivery of speech. This can be a matter of opinion, but it surely can be stated without causing a frenzied uproar.

The main body of criticism was directed at the people who surround the Court and their aloofness from ordinary life and people.

It is no criticism but a fact to say that the education and upbringing of the Queen and Princess Margaret was narrow and restricted, and it should certainly be a matter of concern to see that the Court be broadened to suit the needs of a complex and modern society.

The Press is constantly complaining that Press relations at the Palace are inadequate and antiquated, and all the public seems to get is domestic chit chat and the spectacle of Royalty treated like film stars.

It is amusing to read that Lord Altrincham in Elizabeth I's day would have been sent to the tower, but it is not so amusing to reflect that there are zealots today who are evidently living in the Middle Ages.

There are people alive now who can remember when Royalty was treated to very forthright criticism and not handled as if they were puppets.

Letters, Molly Stuart. I must say that it is rather refreshing to read of Lord Altrincham's candid comments on Royalty. He has only said what a lot of people have been thinking.

The tweedy, horsey set around the Queen are completely out of touch with modern realities, and they only represent one minute fraction of the community.

The next Letter defends all that is British.

Letters, John K Lavett, Royal Society of St. George. The ill-considered attack on the Queen, even if it was not intended as a personal affront, should be immediately halted if so valuable a unifying factor as the Crown is to remain an unsullied force in world affairs.

For Australians, the Crown has special significance as a bond with the great and ancient peoples of the western hemisphere who find, with us, in the Crown a common centre of loyalty and a common sense of honour.

We have seen in many countries the schisms and disintegration which follow the rejection of ancient loyalties and proud traditions. These dangers Britain has escaped, because, while freely accepting reform (even of the most radical kind) she has steadily refused to break with the temporal sanctities of her past – the values summed up and expressed in the monarchy whose origins go back to the House of Wessex and to the first beginnings of Christian civilisation.

From the personal viewpoint, her majesty has given so fine a lead to the citizens of her Commonwealth that she has become Queen of our hearts and minds as well as of our lands and territories.

The discussion went on but with so few new thoughts emerging that I will not quote them. **Except** for the final paragraph of the final Letter, which is so wonderfully vituperative that I wonder that it was actually printed by such a nice paper as the *SMH*.

Letters, J T McGuire. Altrincham's criticisms, not of the Queen, but of the weary hams who write her speeches, set her pace, and protect her from microbes, can hardly be thought unfair nor bitter.

VIEWS OF OVERSEAS TOURISTS

This nation was just starting to be tourist conscious. We had many attractions and a unique attitude to life that was pleasing for tourists to sample. Yet we had many disadvantages. We were a long way from anywhere, and when you got here, it was a big distance to the next place. We had an attitude problem that said that good service to tourists was the same as servility. We also had a backlog in amenities. Our railways, our hotels, roads, our parks and gardens were badly run-down, and our great distances, and small population, were placing a huge burden on our attempts to fix this infrastructure.

Still, tourists did come in small numbers, and locals were waking to the thought that tourism could become an industry, rather than a series of isolated enterprises, and could earn us the dollars that we so badly needed.

We had a long way to go. This Letter below, from an American, gives us a hint of how far.

Letters, John Thompson. I cannot agree with the statement of the Sydney alderman who expressed the view that your hotels "are among the world's finest."

In Los Angeles we are extremely tourist conscious, and we believe if we treat them right they will want to come back. Services provided include heating, of course, in winter and air-conditioning in summer; also round the clock restaurant or coffee shop service, and room service, if desired.

Many motels and auto courts also feature a free Continental breakfast, with swimming pools galore for the aquatic-minded guests. **Rooms with a bathroom** (well equipped with power points) are the rule, rather than the exception, and coin-operated TV and radio are always obtainable. **In many instances the TV service is free.**

In my travels round Sydney I have noticed many buildings at major intersections which are described as hotels, but in actual fact appear to be strictly beer joints with the "guests" spilling over on to the sidewalk.

Certainly if you wish to encourage American tourists your service will have to improve 100 per cent, for pretty beaches will never take the place of real tourist amenities. As one of my countrymen expressed it, "I came too far for too little."

This was a typical Letter from Americans. But there was a **second typical Letter** that stressed the friendliness of the people, if you got on the right side of them.

Letters, Carl Rosenfeld. In reply to your correspondent, John Thompson, I would like to add a word in defence of Australian hotels and restaurants.

During a three weeks' stay there I found that **the better places** compare very favourably with their opposites in America. It is probably true that more such establishments are needed if you want a greater influx of American visitors, and it is probably also true that many places could stand some modernisation. But wherever I have dined or stayed in the last three weeks, I found the personal service of the attendants far more pleasant than what I am used to.

It seemed to me that waiters, porters, clerks took a personal interest in their work and endeavoured to make my stay a pleasant one, without – as in America – making it obvious that their real interest was only in a good tip. They seemed to be pleasantly surprised to receive any tips at all.

I shall return to San Francisco with many fond memories.

Some of the amenities that overseas tourists wanted could easily be fixed. For example, the railways and the pubs could be readily fixed. All it would take would be a **complete change in attitude of those involved, and that could be achieved in a generation or two. And billions of dollars.**

Comment. Happily, I say, this nation has somehow risen to this challenge. We have not reached the giddy heights of some American facilities, and indeed I hope we never do. But, except for some glaring shortfalls, such as our railways, tourists can now rest and visit in most of our facilities and attractions with the same comfort and service that they would get at home.

Another area where Americans had suggestions was in our use of our natural attractions. Most of them flew into **Sydney**, and thought that a 60-mile trip to the Blue Mountains would let them see the outback. So, Katoomba was a popular destination. Anyone who has a morbid liking for gum trees will tell you that, valley after valley,

God's contributions to monotony are there for all to see. Americans liked them, and many wrote that we should exploit them and their valleys.

This was seen as a reasonable idea, but at what cost?

Letters, John Scougall. The move by the Blue Mountains City Council to impose a levy on guests at hotels and guest houses to finance a scheme to improve amenities for tourists in the mountains has aroused much opposition. But so far the only objections raised hinge around the question of who should foot the bill, whereas it seems that there are good reasons to oppose it on more logical grounds.

Your news item reporting the move quotes the mayor, Alderman Murphy, as saying: "There are scores of beautiful valleys which are at present uninhabited, and the money we receive from tourists would be spent on opening them up." This is to me the crux of the whole thing.

We all know that Katoomba leans heavily on the tourist trade for its existence, but there is a limit to the amount of "opening up" that can be done. The beautiful valleys, most of which are accessible only on foot, are one of the main tourist attractions – largely because they are still in their natural state.

One wonders how many trees will fall to the axe if the plans are carried forward. It would be a tragedy if these valleys suffered the same fate as many of the other Blue Mountains areas, such as Springwood and Blaxland, which now have little more to offer in the way of scenic attractions than the closer Sydney suburbs.

Letters, K Collins. How accurate is your correspondent John Scougall when he pinpoints the crux of the matter of "opening up" the Blue Mountains.

After exactly 40 years' association with the mountains, it has become painfully obvious to me that "opening up" means axes and bulldozers to the fore with the resulting roads, no doubt of first-class construction, but eventually leaving a district no more attractive than a Sydney suburb. I suggest that Blue Mountain councillors study the roadwork of the Cambewarra Mountains-Kangaroo Valley district or the Central Coast area between say, Kincumber and Wamberal. There, notwithstanding bitumen roads and telephone and electric-light services, it has been possible to retain the scenic features of those districts.

Comment. Again, **this type of argument was new to Australia. Environmentalists were just now starting to make headway.** Mind you, their voices could scarcely be heard even then. Today, of course, any project, big or small, has to get past numbers of dissident groups before it can get the tick of approval by a dozen authorities. But in 1957, such controls were scarcer, and developments were not subject to much scrutiny at all. On the one hand, this was good. On the other hand, this was bad. But which was which, I leave you to decide.

GAOL WARDERS NOT APPRECIATED

I have been researching and writing these books for **over 14 years**. When it comes to crimes and to court cases, I can remember, off the top of my head, the exploits of Darcy and Dugan, and murderers Robert Ryan and Jean Lee both of whom were executed. Then there was the baffling and unsolved murder of Chandler and McLeod, and the horror of the two beheaded victims at Maitland. This was made all the more gruesome by the mother of one victim discovering one of the heads floating in the Hunter River, 20 miles downstream.

Max Stuart, an Aborigine, was charged in Adelaide with murder, and Rupert Murdoch became an advocate for him. Shirley Bieger waited outside a nightclub with a loaded rifle and shot her boyfriend as he emerged, and was not convicted. Footballer Bobby Lulham was poisoned by his mother-in-law. Dozens of boys and young men, hunting in packs, were sentenced for long, sometimes mandatory, sentences and sent for life to the toughest prisons in the nation to pay for their crime. .

Once the villains among these were imprisoned, they fell out of the limelight. A couple of Letters per year pleaded their cause, but society was generally of the opinion that they deserved what they got.

One group in the community that escaped all notice was the prison warders. Occasionally they got on the front pages when there was a gaol break, or when they staged a short strike. But no one was systematically pleading their cause. The Letter below sets out to do this, but just scratches the surface.

Letters, Charles Mead. The public at large is unfortunately completely uninformed in regard to the difficulties and inconveniences the average warder has to put up with. The man on post duty is underpaid and ill-clad, and his position towards the prisoners is insecure. We are unarmed and hampered by an outdated regulation, dating back to 1894.

If prisoners escape, it is largely due to hopelessly inadequate supervision. There are only 30 warders actually guarding 1,200 prisoners 24 hours a day, seven days a week at £16/10/, but we have 68 people, such as principal warders, senior warders, overseers, clerks, storemen, etc., who draw high wages for an easy 4½ day week, but contribute nothing to the security of the gaol.

Long Bay has become just another "Public Service Department" with all the well-known drawbacks.

We felt that ever since the "food riot" earlier this year, a change in administrative policy was badly needed, and the Comptroller-General, was approached accordingly. The result was that two months ago a large group of prisoners serving long sentences for sex crimes, violence, sadism, and even murder, were permitted to work outside the walls, supervised only by one unarmed warder. These are impossible conditions.

In spite of all these serious handicaps, we try to do our best to protect the public from the consequences of official short-sightedness and mismanagement.

What we need is less administration, but more security and humanity for the prisoners; more responsibility for the warders, and better financial recognition for these few who know how to handle convicts, and who now carry the burden anyway.

NEWS AND VIEWS

How the other half lives. In NSW, farmers in the region of Gloucester have been **plagued by vast hordes of dingoes that live in the State forests,** and come out at nights and eat the calves and sheep and **farm dogs**. The NSW Government has **dropped 20,000 baits** in the area **by aeroplane**....

One grazier said that "it is so serious that we have **erected a wire fence, five feet high, right round our 3,000 acre property**. You can hear them howling all day and night."

SEPTEMBER NEWS ITEMS

The Victorian Cabinet has announced that it intends to allow late night shopping in retail stores one night a week. No other State has allowed this. The argument from the unions is that it places too much stress on workers. And there were other valid arguments against it. On the other hand, **millions of shoppers would welcome it….**

Stirred up by the news from Victoria, about **10 stores in the Sydney seaside suburb of Manly** announced, with publicity, that they would open on Friday night for some hours. **They did that. The response from customers was substantial**, and authorities said that crowds there were the biggest ever, including Christmas. It remains to be seen **if the promised prosecutions are forthcoming.**

Violence is starting to erupt in the southern US states. A Federal Court decision said that **black children would be allowed to attend formerly white schools**. The Governor of Arkansas called out the National Guard **to prevent this** at a place called Little Rock….

In Nashville **a school was dynamited** the night after a white school granted admission to a black boy. Six Birmingham men were arrested on charges of the **kidnapping and mutilation** of a black judge who supported desegregation. Other bashings, the breaking of shop windows, and looting, were reported.

Comment. Sadly, this was just the beginning.

Near the NSW town of Yass, **a father of three** was working in the back shed in the evening. A phone call came for him, and **his wife jogged to the shed to get**

him. Inside the house, a spark from their wood fire jumped the protective grate, and **started a fire which took hold and burned the house down. The three children, aged 5 and under, died in the inferno.**

A prisoner at Melbourne's Pentridge **Gaol attempted to   escape**. He was in prison because he had murdered his sister. **He scaled a barbed-wire fence inside the prison**, ran a hundred yards amid shouts and the blowing of whistles, and then gun shots. He climbed the stone wall round the prison, and **when he was near the top, he was shot and killed**.

This episode was all the more remarkable **because the prisoner was just a lad, aged 14. An enquiry will be held.**

Doc Evatt has survived a motion of no confidence in the Labor Party Caucus. Evatt is not at all popular in his old electorate of Barton, and **he will move to Hunter, the safest Labor seat in the nation. But note that the strife in Labor's ranks still continues....**

Menzies has been safe for seven years, and will be for another ten. And the Liberals will stay in office for another14 years. The moral is that **the electorate will not support a divided party.**

In Little Rock, 1,000 armed paratroopers in full military gear met black children at the railway and marched with them into the school. President Eisenhower said that he had authorised this because **"mob rule threatens the safety of the United States and the free world."**

GIVE NON-BRITS A FAIR GO?

After the war, our first new migrants were from Britain. No one thought that there was any alternative. We at the time were nearly all from British stock, we all had relatives in Britain, and were part of the same great pink Empire. We shared traditions, and monarchy, laws, and a language. So Brits took up our offer of cheap transport, and some job and housing support, and hopped on ships headed for the land of golden opportunity. We, for our part, thought that we needed immigrants, and knew that we needed to populate or perish. So, who better than our related folk from Britain?

By 1957, the situation had changed. The first influx of Brits anxious to get out of Britain at any cost was now over, and so migrants from there were harder to get. But around 1950, we had let in thousands of so-called Poles and Balts, and they had proved to be just as worthy as the Brits.

But they did not have an easy path. Obviously the language made a difference. And in housing and jobs, there were problems for them, because they were seen as taking up positions that should have gone to Aussies. More generally, in society there was always a suspicion of them, a feeling that indeed they were foreign, and a polite acceptance of them but not as true dinky-di Aussies.

The first Letter below conveys some thoughts on this.

Letters, Jan Novak. I wonder if any of your readers could explain to me why immigrants from Britain should necessarily prove to be of better qualities than those from Continental Europe. It seems to me that we should perhaps call a spade a spade and admit that this vocal advocacy of preference for immigrants from

Britain amounts to a plain propaganda of racial hatred leading to nothing less than a state of mutual distrust.

Are we Australians of non-British origin supposed to be so utterly stupid as to help to build a nation of which we should be regarded as second-rate citizens? I fail to appreciate why this country must become a little England or why Australia's servility towards England must remain to be regarded as a cornerstone of our behaviour. Am I to believe that a London Cockney is to be my teacher?

Of course, it would be foolish to break certain traditions, and the fact that this country belongs to the British Commonwealth of Nations is one of the safeguards of the future democratic development of Australia. But there seem to be limits below which a young nation cannot go without becoming servile: instead of becoming a virile young nation we may finish up as a community of sterile colonials whose only pride is to imitate the mother country, right or wrong.

I fail to see why immigrants from Europe should be treated as second-class human beings, and I challenge the wisdom of those who, being apparently ill-informed, try to poison the mutual relations between the citizens of this country and ours.

This brought a quick response.

Letters, A Spiers. Jan Novak's letter must be like a breath of fresh air to those of us imbued with the Australian spirit of "fair go." Let's have more expressions of this kind.

As a works' manager, going back to the early thirties, handling Labor and dealing with management, through depression, hard times, war, postwar and boom times, let me say I found the Australian as good as they come and certainly no worse.

Although statistics figured us predominantly British stock some years back, over the period I mention my contact comprised a cross-section of people whose forbears hailed from all quarters of the world.

There was no shortage of opinions, on both sides. One pointed out that this is a British country, and our loyalty to the Queen was sufficient to end the debate. Another writer claimed that "the British Navy has protected our shores for over a century, and thus we owed Britain gratitude for that." This opinion, so soon after the failure of Britain to help Australia materially in WWII, brought forth a few Letters that said that the only times that our shores have needed protection, it was the Americans we relied on.

A Mrs Graings took the view that we have always resisted invaders from Europe and Asia in this country, and we have almost 100,000 dead and crippled men to show for it. Why, she asks, would we let them come in now, even if they appear to be coming peacefully. They are still invaders.

A number of writers pointed out that Poles, and Czechs and Dutch fought side by side with our soldiers and our airmen in the Battle for Britain. Could these people, and the nations that bore them, be treated like second-class citizens?

The argument waxed backwards and forwards, and it was surprising to me how strong the forces were against the migrants. Ignorance and bigotry were displayed about equally with wisdom. In the final analysis, though, most writers were for accepting Europeans on an equal footing, and the following Letter reflects well their position.

Letters, Carmel McMaugh. Let us once and for all get the immigration position straight. Our migrants are here mainly because we need them. Our Government invited them not, as many of us would like to think, out of Christian charity, but because the economy and potential defence of our country in time of war require a higher population than we are likely to achieve by natural increase.

By all means let our migrants be British, if that is possible, **not** because it has been shown that they are our best-behaved New Australians, **but** because, theoretically, they ought to be easier to assimilate and, therefore, the real strain of assimilation should be felt only in the direction of those of minority racial groups. That there is a strain is obvious from the hurt letters in your columns from non-British migrants and from the bigoted, unkind letters from the pro-British section of our community.

As a sixth generation Australian (of British stock), I resent that attitude which regards England as "home." This country is my home and is to become "home" for our migrants, of British, Italian, Dutch, German and whatever other national origin.

FLUORIDATION, LIKE IT OR NOT

Australians' teeth were less than impressive, and in this period of post-war prosperity, it was thought that remedial measures would gradually make a difference. Overseas, in many parts of many countries, it was observed beyond doubt that whole cities and towns had near perfect teeth, and that this occurred where they drew their drinking water from sources that had fluoride in it. So, in those nations, pressure was growing to fluoridate the drinking water of the whole population.

This movement had come to Australia, and the various Federal and State authorities had concluded that a decision to fluoridate a region's water supply should be made by the local Councils. By 1957, a few Councils had done this, while some of them had outright rejected it. The bulk of Councils were thinking it over.

As you will see below, those in favour of fluoridation thought that citizens should have good teeth, and this was one way to get them. Those opposed thought that the science was problematic, but in any case, that citizens should not be forced to swallow a chemical substance, with no alternative open to them.

There were other arguments, and I give you a sample. The debate was kicked off by a Letter from a Professor Martin at the University of Sydney, and cited studies and statistics from prestigious authorities right round the world that said that fluoride in water supplies was safe, and effective in reducing cavities by 50 per cent.

Next day, another writer quoted another set of facts from other authorities world-wide that stated the substance was dangerous to teeth and to general health. Similar Letters followed, but as usual in public controversies, few of them could be trusted.

More substantial arguments followed.

Letters, A Ferguson. The significant point about the proposal which the professor has ignored is that it is a plan to extend centralised, managerial control over the private lives of citizens in one particular respect, invading the basic faculty, inherent in all forms of life, of selecting the materials taken into the body, as well as the more specifically human right to freedom of choice in so personal a matter.

It must be obvious from the first that a proposal to place in the public water supply a substance, which anyone who can read can discover to be sufficiently toxic for use as rat poison or insecticide, must cause a good deal of reasonable apprehension among the public.

In the present situation of growing uneasiness about the increasing chemical adulteration of food, drink and atmosphere in relation to the increase of chronic disease of unknown origin, it is both irresponsible and damaging to public confidence in the water supply and in the public health services.

One thing is certain: whatever the physical effects of fluoridated water may be (and the matter has by no means received the universal approbation suggested by Professor Martin), the position of those who object to having a daily addition to their toxic intake forced upon them is perfectly reasonable and legitimate.

The only proper action on the part of those who wish to test, or to demonstrate, the value of fluorides during tooth formation is to devote the whole of their energies to finding a suitable method of administering the treatment (with consent to those who are expected to benefit and to them only).

Letters, V Kelly. A point omitted by Prof. Martin is that dental caries are not contagious. No water supply authority has any legal or moral right to prescribe medicinally for the health of its customers. Its function is to supply them with potable drinking water.

Prof. Martin admits that "there are still aspects of fluoridation which are not completely understood." This is all the more reason why the public should oppose all attempts to introduce the deadly poison fluoride into their drinking water.

Comment.   This debate is still alive.   For example, in the fifties and sixties, NSW Councils mostly accepted the chemical, while most Queenslanders rejected it. The same mixed results were found round Australia. Though, on the whole, most accepted it. Still, even now 60 years later, there are Councils who are considering reversing their earlier decision.

WE NEED AN ANTHEM

Now, let's get this straight. Every other nation in the world has a national anthem. They play it at all military events, and all sporting events, sometimes at pageants and parades. People stand and look solemn and proud when they hear it, and Americans obviously have trouble with their hearts. We too have similar emotions. Our trouble is that, here we are in 1957, in a nation founded 169 years ago, and **we still don't know what our national anthem is**.

Let me fall back on some correspondence to get the ball rolling.

The following Letter does not like Waltzing Matilda at all, and resolves our difficulty by suggesting that we need not one, but two national anthems.

Letters, Oscar Walters, Hon. Sec., Australian National Anthem Quest. Most Australians know, or should, that "God Save the Queen" is primarily Australia's National Anthem, but all true Australians know, or should know, that we are sadly lacking in a National Anthem subsidiary to "God Save the Queen" for use on occasions of **purely Australian significance**.

Nevertheless, Australia should look upon this question in a very deep sense and not just to satisfy the whims of any particular section of public thought.

With regard to "Waltzing Matilda," I feel its origin is of no value whatever, for surely nobody with the slightest appreciation of the dignity which must be embodied in a National Anthem would consider the use of this tune for this purpose.

There is only one democratic way of determining what should be Australia's anthem, and that is by public plebiscite.

Letters, (Mrs) Joan Macfarlan. But I feel a public plebiscite for which he asks, would show that "Waltzing Matilda" is the Australian theme song, at home and abroad. Admittedly the words needs revising, swagmen and jumbucks being obsolete terms nowadays. I understand fine new words were used to the "Waltzing Matilda" tune at the Olympics last year?

Recently, in places as far apart as Bulawayo, Khartoum, Baghdad, Madrid and New Orleans, "Waltzing Matilda" was played in my honour by the hotel orchestras (presumably after inspecting the hotel registers to ascertain guests' nationalities). In every case it was immediately realised that an Australian was visiting.

Surely this is proof that the song has world-wide recognition as distinctly "ours" -- why try to alter it, whatever its origin?

With that as background, I now commend this Letter below. You might not agree with anything or everything he says, but it is all worth thinking about.

Letters, M Frame. I have heard all sorts of suggestions over the years about a national anthem. Before I make any suggestions on this, let me voice a question that needs discussion. **Should we, or anyone, have a national anthem?**

I will leave aside the advantages that people propose. You have probably heard them often. Let me **make a point against anthems**. It is that they are used for celebrating at some grand national events or occasions, and to that point are not objectionable. But at other times, **they play on people's emotions so as to lift them to passions and hatred of others**. Hitler generally used music to further his indoctrination and particularly the national anthem. The USA does the same on every possible occasion to raise its citizens into a fervour of patriotism. Most nations do exactly the same.

What I am saying is that anthems have a good purpose in helping the nation come together for ethical purpose. But **anthems also have their dark side**, and their exploitation can be truly evil.

Leaving that aside, if you will permit me, **I will now comment on Australia's anthem**. As to *God Save the Queen*, its words are obsolete and innocuous. It is not fit for Australia, and if our migration program continues as it is now doing, it will become even more obsolete. Its one, insignificant, advantage is that it can be brief.

One alternative is *Waltzing Matilda*. What silly words it has. It uses arcane words, and after four laborious verses, points out that crime does not pay. It **does** have a ditty that is reminiscent of old Irish ditties, and to that extent it is acceptable. But not so acceptable as to become a national anthem. Its one advantage is that it is recognised as Australian, and should be reserved for overseas use, at parties and trivial and fun-filled occasions.

The existing *Advance Australia Fair* is fair enough. It is pompous or regal, its words are jingoistic, and it can be brief. It fits the bill for an anthem. **It has my vote.**

I have seen attempts in the past to get a different anthem. I can remember a push to use something from the Eureka Stockade, and equally ridiculous, in the late 1930's, the *Workers' Flag*. But any move to change just splits the nation, and we all get down to endlessly supporting the theme we first thought of.

I would like to see us cut the cackle, and accept *Australia Fair,* and get on with thinking about things worth thinking about.

MICHAEL SAWTELL AND ABORIGINES

Foreword. I am nearly at the end of writing this series of books, so I will take the opportunity to mention a correspondent who has been an inspiration to me. For 14 years, I have plugged away at the daily newspapers for the 32-year period from 1939 to 1970. For most of this time, one gentleman, Michael (Olaf) Sawtell has been my constant companion. He has had a Letter published in the *SMH* at least every month and often more frequently. This in itself is a rare feat, given that most writers never get their Letters published. But on top of that, all of his Letters have been sensible, an even greater feat, and cogent.

His general theme was the Australian outback, and the Aborigines in particular. Below, he is at his best, taking up a recurring theme of alcohol and the Aborigines.

Letters, Michael Sawtell, Aborigines' Welfare Board of NSW. In commenting on your very sensible leading article about lifting Section 9 of the Act and allowing persons of Aboriginal blood to enter the hotels, I must confess that I do not know quite where I stand, for I know so much about the problem from all aspects.

From 1949, when the then Chief Secretary, Mr Clive Evatt, tried the experiment of allowing Aborigines to enter the hotels, I was very strongly in the opposition, and the police supported me. I think the police still would, and we must respect their opinion, for they are the men who have to deal with drunken Aborigines.

Booze is perhaps the greatest problem in Aboriginal welfare. However, it must be understood that in New South Wales many of those people who are called Aborigines are nearly white. Drinking Aborigines give all the Aborigines in any district a bad reputation. They also get thousands of pounds behind in their rent-purchase houses.

The Aborigines' Welfare Board of New South Wales has continually warned persons of Aboriginal blood that they cannot expect to be accepted into any decent society while they booze and behave badly. Then again most of those Aborigines are members of unions and are expected to fight in wartime, and to them full citizenship means the right to breast the bar with their fellow-unionists.

Then again, as you rightly say, many publicans may refuse to serve Aborigines. I know several who would not serve Aborigines. However, no matter what we do the Aborigines will still get black-market plonk. So it may be as well to lift Section 9 and hope for the best.

Comment. Sawtell's advocacy of Aborigines was not the only one, but it was pretty lonely in 1957. It was only 10 years later that the general population started to realise what a rotten deal they were getting, and began the long process – still ongoing – of repairing the damage.

HORSEMEAT

I can't keep you in suspense any longer. I know you have been dying waiting for any news on horsemeat, so now that it has come to me, I am happy to deliver it to you without further comment.

Letters, R Webb. Apparently dog and pet shops have a free hand in deciding what charge will be made for horsemeat. Prices vary from 1/4 a pound in Redfern up to 1/7 a pound in Rockdale and 1/8 a pound in Hurstville, quite a difference for a common item.

Service and civility decrease as the price increases, and to ask for greaseproof wrapping is a certain means of upsetting the dearer shopkeepers.

Letters, Eve Jillett. All cat and dog owners will share the concern expressed by R Webb about the dearness of horsemeat. But rises in the price would be more acceptable if the quality were dependable.

Recently I bought 6lb. So much of it was gristly and tough that it could not be cut up into sufficiently small pieces to serve to the animals. This inedible portion weighed 6lb.

I returned it to the shop but could get no redress from the manager. Isn't this a matter in which the health and the price authorities should show a livelier interest?

NEWS AND VIEWS

National Service for young men is being wound down. As part of this, the 19th Battalion at **Holsworthy camp will hold a ceremonial parade for its mascot**, a goat, now named Corporal Vanguard. The goat entered service as a rookie private, and was soon found to be "efficient" and hence his promotion to corporal. After the parade, to be attended by the full camp, **the corporal will be transferred to the reserve**.

OCTOBER NEWS ITEMS

Rail systems round the nation are being upgraded. **The old coal-fired locos are being replaced with diesels**, and some country lines, adjacent to the major cities, **are being electrified**. So, if you are a train spotter, you had better look sharp.

A US nuclear submarine broke all records with a trip to England of 5,000 miles in which it stayed below the surface **for 14 days**. **Who said that nuclear power would not be used for peaceful purposes?**

October 6th. **Russia** jumped ahead in the space race with America **by launching Sputnik, the first man-made satellite, into orbit**. The Russians were jubilant though the response from the US was muted, even grudging. A prominent Senator could only say "this will result in a stepping up of the cold war, with Russia throwing its weight round even more…."

The Professor of Physics at Sydney University, well-known **Harry Messel, said that this could mean "the extinction of civilisation"** if Russia could somehow use the technology to dominate the world. "It is a magnificent scientific feat but **I have the feeling we are nearing the end….**"

The next night, tens of thousands of people in the eastern States of this nation excitedly **watched as the satellite moved across the sky** from south to north. On each orbit, it was in view for about ten minutes, cloud permitting….

Up till now, the reports of Russian scientific achievements had been poo-paahed by the USA and its allies. Now they had to be taken seriously, and this included their earlier claim that **they had missiles capable of flying to other continents**. This was **a great propaganda victory for them**, but scary for their enemies.

October 12th. **The Queen** is touring Canada. Today, she gave **her first televised speech** "in English and fluent French."

In San Marino, the tiny Republic on Italy's border, the ruling **Communist Party lost its majority** and was sent to the dust heap. Its members thought they **could regain power by crippling the new government with a general strike**, which they called for on October 14....

The new government, in a flash of brilliance, **made that day a public holiday**. This completely "took the wind out of the sails of the Reds, and for the moment the new government is secure." **What a clever government.**

In the NSW country town of Bega, a man was dissatisfied with the local constable. **He placed a 6-gallon milk-can full of dynamite on the constable's verandah, and ignited it. It exploded and killed the constable and his wife and daughter.** The man admits the act, and says **he just wanted to frighten the policeman**. He will be sentenced in a few days.

It's official. Our statistics show that Australians in 1957 were **living 12 years longer than in 1907.**

SPUTNIK

The launching of the Russian satellite was not good news for the USA. It had for years been saying how advanced they were in all things, and how backward the Communists were. Now, for all the world to see, the Reds had jumped ahead in the most obvious race that existed, and the world suddenly started to believe all their claims that were discredited before.

In Australia, the average citizen was impressed. For weeks, thousands and thousands of people went out at night to see the satellite cruise the sky. **Probably most of them still remember their first sighting**, and the feeling of wonder that went with it. The ordinary man and woman were both impressed and laudatory.

Letters, E Moody. Sputnik may well prove to be the best ambassador yet for the promotion of world peace and understanding.

This indisputable scientific victory has won for the Russians a world respect hitherto denied them.

In the past we have belittled their claims, scorned the quality of their goods and denounced their methods. Undoubtedly this has been a powerful factor in earning their hostility, and strengthening their determination to outdo us.

Fortunately, they have been able to demonstrate their scientific and technological equality, if not supremacy, with a peaceful device. Now, basking in their new-found aura of world respect, there is every possibility that they will concentrate their talents on similar harmless but all-absorbing projects in friendly rivalry with the rest of the world's scientists.

Some of them wanted the praise to be spread even further.

Letters, Edmund Brian. There is no denying that the Russian satellite is a wonderful achievement, but I think a little reflection on the matter is necessary, in order to see things in the correct perspective.

We have seen how the launching of this small object into the unknown has caused a great deal of astonishment. I wonder why all the huge planets, stars, and the brilliant moon, infinitely greater, have not caused even more excitement and why the Creator of all this does not get more homage.

Others could see that the world might benefit.

Letters, John Devenney. Since the launching of the Russian satellite Sputnik the thing that has impressed me most is the good-natured and sportsmanlike manner in which the fact has been accepted by most Australians, including the newspapers.

If this same good-natured attitude were to prevail at all times, on all occasions, throughout the world, I feel sure that we could look forward to many years of international peace.

Among public figures, governments, churches and the Press, grudging acceptance of the Russian feat was given. The most vocal group at this time were the scientific community, and most of the comments were of the "I told you so" type, and took the form of an argument for more money for science and maths in the schools and universities.

Professor Gutman from a University in Sydney was happy to scourge himself and others. He wrote

Letters, (Dr) Felix Gutman, NSW University of Technology. The recent brilliant technological successes achieved by Soviet Russia forebode only ill for the free world's chances in what Moscow calls "peaceful competition."

For this we, as a community, have only ourselves to blame; we are now reaping the first fruit of our consistent neglect of the scientist, of research, of the universities.

Any noteworthy research carried out in Australian universities has been, and is being, done only in the face of most formidable difficulties, and in spite of grossly inadequate financial support.

He suggested a solution that involved extra pay for scientists, and more science money **for the universities**. The President of the NSW Teachers' Federation wanted the extra funding to go to recruiting more science graduates for teaching science in **High Schools**. After that, the discussion degenerated into armed camps arguing whether **the French language** was more important than science. You might expect correctly that nothing of substance came from this.

Comment. Sputnik kept moving round its orbit, but in Australia it soon became a fizzer. People still watched at night, and got a great deal of fun from finding it in the sky. But in the heavy-weight world of our decision makers and opinion leaders, it appeared to be something that no one wanted to talk about. **Maybe the US would be able to trump the Sputnik act. Until then, Mum's the word.**

ATOMIC REACTOR ACCIDENT

Since the dropping of the A-bombs on Japan twelve years ago, the world had been fearful of further nuclear events. There was the terrible slaughter caused by the explosion itself, then the immediate and delayed effects of radiation. There was also the possibility of mutations, and the damage to the environment, and even **the possibility of the extinction of the human race** in a nuclear war.

Now a new threat emerged, from Britain. A few weeks ago, weaknesses occurred in the filtration of released gasses from a nuclear reactor in the region of Cumberland. No one was hurt, but the release of radio-active particles of iodine was high enough to cancel the production of milk in the area. Assurances were given all round that new equipment meant that no such event could happen in the future, but the general fear of nuclear technology meant that many fears were not allayed.

The *SMH* did a feature article on the faults at the British plant, so new worries were added to the local distrust. An official representative of the British Atomic Energy Authority tried to set our minds at rest.

J B Richardson, UK Atomic Energy Authority in Australia. First, it should be reiterated that the accident could only occur in an air-cooled open-circuit pile, and could not occur at Calder Hall or at any of the power stations now under construction for the electricity authorities. There is no need at all for the public to lose confidence in the vast atomic power program in Britain or elsewhere.

It is also desirable to deny reports that have tended to give an impression as to the finding of strontium 90 in the area. It must be emphasised that checks for strontium 90 have been made, and the highest levels reported are still only between one-fifth and one-tenth of that which would be safe for lifetime consumption.

Tests have been carried out and are continuing on Thirlmere Water and other bodies of water in the area (lakes in Lakeland). The levels of radio-activity revealed by these measures are less than 1/100th of the levels agreed by the International Commission for Radiological Protection as safe for human consumption.

Comment. It was reassuring information, and not to be dismissed lightly. But the fact remains that **since then** there have been several very serious explosions and incidents in nuclear plants world-wide. Though I must admit I have no information on how the nuclear power industry stacks up against the traditional coal-fired industry in terms of killing people and destroying lives.

THE BEST ON THE MENU

An article in the *SMH* on Australia's diet stirred many readers to comment. Most agreed that our traditional breakfast menu of sausage, bacon and eggs, with perhaps a chop, was most unexciting. A few more thought that the evening meal of a quarter pound steak with mashed potatoes and some boiled cabbage was not much to look forward to.

One writer weighed in some with good suggestions. He strayed from the menu items a bit, but his wisdom is profound.

Letters, T C Andrews. Several statements in a recent article in the "Herald" entitled "Why not vary our monotonous diet?" by John Goode, are incorrect. First, I have cooked and eaten kangaroo meat a few times, but I have never attempted to bake it, and neither do our Aborigines attempt to bake it.

They may singe it in open fire, but there's only one way to cook roo meat, and that is by steaming it. Cooked in this way it has one fault, and that is there is never enough left over for a second helping. Therefore the proof of the steamer is in the eating.

Mr Goode's pride of native dishes is baked snake. I know how he arrived at this decision: it is because he has never tasted baked bandicoot cooked native fashion. This dish also has the same fault attached to it as the kangaroo meat. Place sucking pig and baked bandicoot on the table before a diner and do not tell him which is which. I'll lay a wager the sucking pig is left on the table.

His second choice is the Australian water rat. I take it he means the Hydromys Chrysogaster Lutrilla. With a name like that it should be good eating. If he does mean this animal, he is a little astray when he describes it as a vegetable-eater.

This is what the Australian Museum has to say about it: The rat sometimes called the beaver rat, originally named by Sir William Macleay in 1863. Its food consists of fresh water mussels, snails, yabbies, frogs, water birds and their eggs.

The specimen I caught, which is now in the museum, weighed 1lb 14oz, length overall 25 inches, head and body 13 inches, with a 12-inch tail, black and white like a ringtail. While I had it in confinement it lived on crabs, leather-jackets, and hairy mussels. Some rat.

MISSING THE TRAMS

Letters, B Hooke. It seems to me Castlereagh and Pitt Streets are now ruined with diesel oil fumes from the buses.

On a still, hot morning like this morning (Monday), it was impossible to avoid the fumes. It would be good if the latter could be destroyed before poisoning the atmosphere. I miss the trams.

BRING OUT A BRIT

At the moment, the number of British migrants was decreasing, and their place was being taken by Europeans. Some people thought that British stock would improve the nation, and wanted us to have the bluest blood possible. So there were a number of private groups mustering members who would pay for the fare of migrant families, and provide a job and housing for them when they got here.

Letters, Marjorie Unger. Anglicans are urged by Dr Mowll to support the "Bring Out a Briton" campaign. Whilst many would like to give practical recognition to this urgent need, individual sponsorship is impossible for them.

Their interest should be harnessed in some cooperative effort. Perhaps each parish committee could aim to buy a suitable house in its own district. In this way a new migrant family could be accommodated, say, every six months. Such a scheme would attract the best types and their employment should present no difficulties.

This is but one suggestion. There must be many effective ways open to those Anglicans who care.

DISGUSTING HABIT

Letters, J A Robson. If some motorists must indulge in the disgusting habit of spitting from their moving cars, may I, through your columns, ask these people to use their rear vision mirrors to make quite sure there is no other car within range before they do so.

Comment. Spitting was far too common. Footpaths also took their fair share of spit. It is much less of a problem now. Recent research suggested that this was as a result of the decrease in smoking, especially roll-your-own.

EROSION AND GRAZING

This Letter stems from an ongoing dispute between farmers, various Lands Departments, and sundry Preservation Authorities. They were arguing about whether grazing should be allowed on public lands that bordered on the Great Dividing Range. This land was bare in the colder months, but grew luscious grass in the summer when it was warmer.

There is no point in going into detail here. It would take pages, and it was all in flux anyway. This Letter below gives a minute sample of the correspondence that was being generated in the Press and elsewhere.

Letters, Lindsay Ashton. We must all be grateful to the Minister for Lands, Mr Nott, for a new conception of soil conservation.

For generations, we have been misled into believing that vegetation binds the soil and prevents erosion. Mr Nott has now made it clear that uncontrolled growth leads to bushfires, which promote erosion.

From now on, the solution is simple. Destroy all forests, scrub and even long grass, anything capable of burning. Then introduce grazing over the whole State, regardless of altitude or slope. There would certainly be no more bushfire hazard, and presumably no more erosion.

All of which goes to show that in politics, as in mathematics, it is possible to prove anything if you are prepared to ignore commonsense, expert advice and the good of the nation.

CARTONS OR BOTTLES

Letters, Lucie Barnes. The latest development in the milk industry is that the carton is appearing in ever greater numbers among the milk bottles.

Have any efforts been made to ascertain the wishes of the housewife on this change? Many people do not like any food in a carton, certainly not milk.

A question that arises is: Why is it that the cartonned milk is dearer than the bottled milk, since the carton is cheaper to produce, and, while it may only be used once, it requires no washing, as does the bottle?

Comment. Another reader pointed out that glass bottles had to be returned to the factory, while cartons did not. She thought the cost of doing this was substantial, and that this was an argument in favour of cartons.

A DOCTOR STIRS THE POT

A few months after the Suez crisis, all the excitement had died down. But this intrepid doctor still had a point to make.

Letters, (Dr) C B Heald. Having left England for Sydney in the middle of the Suez crisis, one is now sufficiently far removed to be able to realise certain medical factors that have received little or no notice in the Press of the world, yet are of vital importance to all, wherever they live.

The medical fitness and history of the three figures who stood at the apex of the crisis, Eden, Eisenhower and Dulles, is to me – who pioneered the biannual medical examinations of pilots and standards for these – incredible.

Sir Anthony Eden is known to have had no less than three operations in the region of his gall bladder, cystic and common bile ducts, the last one of extreme difficulty and hazard – all these within three years.

President Eisenhower's history is little, if at all, better.

A coronary thrombotic attack, however clear the present electro-cardiogram may be, still remains a past coronary event. Then follow this shortly with an emergency abdominal operation and further trauma. It will be unanimously agreed throughout the medical profession that such a history must leave permanent scars and defects; especially in anyone who has been subjected for years to the burdens of high positions.

Lastly take Mr Dulles. There was a carcinoma of the bowel going forward to acute obstruction, at first misdiagnosed as an appendix, necessitating an extensive emergency operation. Then within weeks, almost days, this patient is once more vitally influencing world policy.

These are the clinical facts. My argument is that the "owners" of such past histories, and at such ages, have quite enough, under the most restful circumstances of living, with which to contend, that **they cannot be sufficiently physically fit to meet the responsibilities of high office**, that their judgments and mental balance are liable to be warped under stress, that they cannot be trusted to hold firmly to a course, and are liable to go off at "half-cock" and are then over-committed. Chief of all, perhaps, their sense of humour and proportion must be "off balance." What else could one expect?

If, after a serious crash, it were found the chief pilot had a history even faintly resembling those quoted, there would be an intense public outcry, and rightly. Yet here we were in 1956 with three chief national pilots, only half physically fit, allowed to carry on.

Comment. I can't work out whether the good doctor is serious. And I can't work out whether the point he raised is a good one or not. **On the one hand**, you could argue that medical aliments certainly **do** have a bad effect on reasoning and mental stability. **On the other**, it could be argued that after a certain age, most people have some chronic or acute ailment. Should most of the population be barred from office or from decision-making on that account? Do younger people have the wisdom and steadiness to make balanced decisions? What do you think?

NOVEMBER NEWS ITEMS

TV in Australia was new, only a few months old. So all sorts of new experiences were being offered. This year, **the Melbourne Cup will be broadcast for the first time**. Note though, before you race to turn on your sets, that it will not be shown live, but **you will have to wait till the evening news to watch it….**

The Victoria Racing Club, which owns the rights to the clip, will **not charge the TV stations to view it**. In return, the stations will promote the race through their channels….

Also, **Movietone and Cinesound newsreels** will receive it on the same basis. **Question.** Remember when newsreels were shown at all picture theatres weekly?

Another question. Can you imagine how much the channels would pay **for the viewing rights today**?

November 4th. Those crafty Russians have done it again. On the 40th anniversary of the Russian Revolution, **they have launched another Satellite, much bigger than Sputnik I. But, this time they have added a special feature. There is a dog on board….**

This dog, called Laika, has already made some rocket flights, and is specially trained for the on-board atmosphere of the satellite. **It will be projected out from the craft in a few days** in a special container, and when it gets close to earth**, it will be pushed out and parachuted to earth to a rendezvous point….**

Sadly, the dog probably died from hunger. Despite the plans, the satellite's batteries lasted only a week.

News of the dog dried up. The Russians told the world in 2002 that she had **died from heat during take-off**.

The NRMA in NSW has introduced a new service, available to all members. It has graded country hotels according to a star rating with the best hotel getting four stars. Only seven hotels got four stars. There were 112 with the lowest rating of one star....

To get a single star, the hotel had to offer a **fair** level of comfort, a guest lounge, adequate lighting and heating, and clean **communal** bathing and toilet facilities....

There was an estimated total of at least 3,000 hotels that did not rate a single star.

New regulations were being promulgated in the nation's big cities that **promised motorists that they would be towed away** if they parked for too long in defined areas. This was, we were told, for **the benefit of the most motorists.**   And certainly it was **never for revenue-raising purposes.**

The new Davis Cup squad was announced, and it looks a bit weak without the now-pros Rosewall and Hoad. There were five players selected, including Mal Anderson, Roy Emerson, and Mervyn Rose. Rod Laver just missed out. **Comment.** I am surprised that Laver got so close. **Everyone knows that left-handers can't play tennis.**

The Japanese Prime Minister will pay a two-day **visit to Australia.** He will be **officially received by the Government. Others however, might not be so quite so cordial.**

REPORTS ON 10 O'CLOCK CLOSING

In the lead-up to the 1956 Olympic Games, all States had considered their stance concerning 6 o'clock closing for hotels, and several had held referenda on the matter with very different results. NSW for example had opted for 10 o'clock closing, with an hour's break in trading from 6.30 pm. Victoria had clearly voted for no extension of drinking hours after 6pm.

In States where later closing was allowed, the general consensus over a few years was that most people approved of the effects. But there were still different opinions.

Letters, (Rev) R Meyer. On the day that you published a report that Police Commissioner Delaney was praising the effect of 10 o'clock closing in New South Wales to a New Zealand audience, I had an interesting experience which I believe has some relevance to the issue in question.

A young married woman with two small children whom I had married years ago, came and told me a story of her husband's neglect, cruelty, improvidence and continual drunkenness, culminating in infidelity and desertion. This of course, is a pattern with which social workers are all too familiar.

When I asked her at what stage of the marriage the heavy, constant drinking began, the answer was unequivocal: "Since 10pm closing."

As one who is constantly faced with these tragic problems, I would like to point out, for the benefit of Mr Delaney and the New Zealand public, that this too is becoming a pattern reply from the unfortunate victims of the 10pm closing legislation.

Letters, Sane Drinker. The Rev Meyer thinks that the experience he had with one young married woman refutes Commissioner Delaney's report on 10 o'clock closing?

My husband, though by no means a drunkard, likes to drink with his mates after work. As we live in an outer suburb, before 10 o'clock closing, he used to drink near his work place and drink very fast to get "his quota" before 6 o'clock. Four nights out of five he would be late home for tea, the children would be in bed and tempers would be frayed.

Now he comes straight home from work. This summer, for the first time since we were married, we have had our own vegetables and odd jobs have been done, as it has been light enough to do these things. The idea was that he would go out after tea for a drink, but, except for weekends, he does not bother going out and the children and I have benefited by having a family circle.

At the weekends, when we can get a neighbour to baby-sit, I go out with him to a family hotel where there is entertainment and in my presence and that of other married people like ourselves, the men do not over-indulge.

In my own street there are many who have the same story to tell.

The confirmed drunkard and alcoholic will get drink no matter what it costs. Why should the moderate civilised drinker suffer because of the few who over-indulge.

Before 10 o'clock closing it was the worker who was penalised. If one had money, the nightclubs sold drink till all hours.

Comment. This matter continued to be argued for decades. Over a period of 60 years, the situation has changed very much, and there are so many different angles to this that any interested party can find a drum to beat and come up with an apparently winning argument. That is, until someone else starts drumming.

To me it is obvious that drinking has become more comfortable and civilised over that period. Less of it now happens in the pubs, and more recently, the club patronage has fallen off a lot. A big part of this has been the introduction of traffic rules that crack down hard on drivers over the limit. Another factor was the opening of TABs so that people could gamble from their lounges at home. So now drinking **in the home, for males and females,** has increased greatly.

I have no idea if the per-person consumption has increased or decreased. I suppose only the vendors of alcohol, and their workers, would hope that it had. But in any case, back in the 1950's, the main aim of liquor reform was to eliminate **the pig-like swill from the pubs** round the nation at various times. **There can be no doubt that this has gone. So that the reforms made then appear to have worked.**

There is always a "but". But were the changed conditions caused by the legislation **then**, or were they caused by other factors **later**, like drink-driving laws or the opening of TABS? **That** remains a matter for conjecture. **What do you think?**

LESSONS FROM TWO ANIMAL STORIES

The human race rather grandly claims that it is given stewardship over all earthly things by one or other of its gods. As a result, the animal kingdom is forced into the back seat. Yet there are lessons we can learn from even the simplest animal event.

LESSON 1. This little episode occurred on the Dorisvale property on the Daly River, close to Darwin.

Press report. The trouble began when a farm dog cornered a wallaby on the bank of a billabong near the homestead. The dog's frantic barking attracted the manager's wife, who rushed outside in time to see the wallaby grasp the dog in it paws and plunge into the billabong.

The wallaby fought with the dog and held its head under water to try to drown it. Mrs Moar grabbed a stick and plunged into waist-deep water to try to save the dog. She was only a few yards from the fighting animals when she turned around to see a big crocodile swimming towards her.

The crocodile swept past her and seized the wallaby, which released the dog.

The crocodile and its victim disappeared into the depths of the billabong. Mrs Moar scrambled from the water, closely followed by the dog.

MORAL. *Always take a wallaby with you when you go swimming in a billabong.*

LESSON 2. A truck-driver captured a "porcupine" while on a week-end pig-shooting trip. Rather cleverly, he named it Porky. He brought it home and, as you would expect, released it in a pub in Sydney's Bankstown.

The frightened creature scampered behind a bar, and the two barmaids climbed screaming on top of that bar. It then buried itself behind some beer pipes and bottles of stout. The humans tried to dislodge him by wrapping him with canvas around his gills, but Porky responded by rolling himself into a ball and refusing to budge.

Then they tried to lever him out using an iron crowbar, a stick, a feather duster, and a shovel. They also tried to smoke him out using matches, but the floor caught alight, and they had to put it out using schooners of water.

They telephoned the zoo, and were advised to "try a raw egg." Half an hour later, the egg was gone, but Porky was still there, all rolled up.

Finally, a Herald reporter, equipped with gardening gloves, dragged him out by a hind foot. Cheers went up, and drinks were shouted all round.

Moral. *Porcupines remain stoutly aloof when fed raw eggs in pubs.*

Post Script. The reporter sent Porky to the zoo and, a month later, told an anxious audience that it was doing just fine.

HOT WATER FROM THE SUN

Letters, Arthur Neve. I have just signed, with considerable reluctance, a large cheque for electricity, with the dismal certainty that, unless I do something about it, the next one will probably be larger. More than half the current used has run down the sink or through the bath plug in the form of hot water.

I cannot understand why, in "sunny Australia," more use is not made of solar heat – the cost of which has not risen since time began. When correctly designed, a solar heater is remarkably efficient. Even an experimental unit I built for my home in Melbourne some years ago gave water far too hot for baths – averaging 120 degrees F in summer.

It is an ideal "do-it-yourself" job, only requiring the services of a plumber to make the connection to the service pipe. Yet, after contacting more than a dozen

Sydney plumbers I found that not one of them had ever seen such a unit.

My last electricity bill should be the biggest I shall have to pay for many years. I have ordered the piping (no costly mirrors are needed to concentrate the heat) and within the next few weeks I hope to have my own hot water system, powered by the sun.

Comment. A few days later, Mr Neve had another Letter published that said he had been deluged for details of his heater, and that he regretted he could not reply to everyone, but he would send the design in roneoed form as soon as he could arrange for this.

PLUTO IN THE SKY

The official response to Sputnik II was no more generous than to the first. But, for persons in the street, it was even more impressive. In particular, the idea of a dog hurtling round above us, and the anticipated drama of her rescue had people everywhere talking and gesticulating towards the planets. The Chinese, we were told often, would change this year to be The Year of the Dog.

For the first few days, excitement was great. Then as the days ticked by, and there was no news, concern for the fate of the dog grew, and it finally died out altogether after a week or so.

In the meantime, people had their say. Protesters at Buckingham Palace and the White House cried out against cruelty to animals. A pack of big dogs paraded outside the UN headquarters in New York, bearing signs that said "Send up Kruschchev", "Dog in danger", and "What did dogs do to earn starvation."

Of course, back here in Oz, the Letter writers were out in force.

Letters, Phyllis M Walsh. In the insane scramble for scientific "advancement," protests against the callous cruelty of the Russians in consigning a defenceless animal to a horrible and prolonged doom are not likely to receive much recognition from scientists of any nation.

Nevertheless, decent human beings are sickened by such inhumanity, and the sooner some of the bright, scientific boys substitute themselves for the animals, the better. If this is advancement, give us back the dark ages!

Letters, Would Be Space Dog. I protest at the degrading spectacle of placarded dogs picketing the UN Headquarters, a picture of which you publish in this morning's "Herald." It is clear to me that the dogs who lent themselves to this cheap stunt must be well below average canine intelligence, and in all probability were unable to read the slogans they bore; or at any rate did not grasp their significance.

As a dog myself, I should like to say that I am proud that one of us is making this historic journey into space, contributing to the sum total of human knowledge. I think I speak for all of us when I say that we would far rather do something useful like our brave comrade Limonchik than make a public exhibition of ourselves in circuses, sideshows, etc., for the profit of some individual. I am proud to be an Australian.

Letters, Paul E Royle. I think that if the people who are making such an outcry were sincere in their love of animals some of them would take a trip to the Prince Edward Dog Home and adopt some lovely dog that otherwise will meet its end ingloriously in the lethal chamber.

Letters, Alison Griffiths. Such moving indignation over the fate of one dog in a Russian satellite. Is not this touching concern disproportionate when we consider the fate of so many Hungarians in another Russian satellite? How much thought is given to their sufferings?

Letters, M Pinney. There surely can be no comparison between animals slaughtered for food, or used in medical research, and the wretched dog dying in space in order that Man may inflict himself upon other planets.

Letters, E M Stephenson. From immemorial time, the dog has been a loyal and faithful friend to man. That widespread sympathy and regret is being shown by mankind in every nation, including Russia, indicates that we are at least conscious of our faithlessness. This small flicker of kindness should surely not be jeered at. Shall we congratulate ourselves that in the near future we shall be able to take our quarrelsome, faithless natures to some planet which has up to now lived in peace and happiness?

Letters, P Fry. Since the fact that the Russians are killing a dog while trying out their new toy is so important, it might be as well to point out that it is not very long since the Americans killed 50,000-odd Japanese in doing much the same thing.

Letters, A Barr. The Christian conscience is awakened in pity for a single dog. The same conscience howls from the house-tops in protest if a brutal murderer is to be hanged.

Where is the Christian conscience when millions, including prisoners of war of several nations, political prisoners of the Soviet Union, etc., are allowed to experience a living death in the economic interests of the Communist leaders in Russia?

Letters, F Dent. It is, indeed, surprising to read Dame Mary Gilmore's letter in regard to the sacrifice of the dog for the good of humanity.

The scientists tell us life in outer space is only possible in space suits -- that there is no life on the planets. What good, then, is the conquest of space to humanity? Landing on the moon in space suits and containers can only be a super stunt, or a war achievement.

Comment. The launching of the two Sputniks, including the sacrifice of the dog, was the event of the year 1957. As I pointed out, not so much for our leaders who were so involved in the Cold War that they could scarcely acknowledge this great Russian feat. But for the ordinary citizens of the world, there was great excitement, and anyone who left their warm beds to watch the display has never forgotten the sightings.

But, lest we get too excited, there is another very different and down-to-earth view of outer space.

Letters, Down With The Sputniks. The brains which have created Sputniks undoubtedly could create forces capable of annihilating whole countries. To counter this grave possibility, the Western Democracies, alas, have no apparent means of offence other than an odd lot of self-destroying intercontinental ballistic missiles, Presleys, Satchmos, Teddy Boys, Mansfields, rock'n'rollers, and Dors.

But, there is one positive way of defeating the odious machinations of the Russians and that is by transferring the whole lot of them to Australia. In this salubrious paradise, they would soon be robbed of all harmful potential as in no time they would be perpetually on strike and so indoctrinated by the Australian cult of Beer, Betting, and Beaches that they would have neither the time nor the inclination, and certainly not the energy, to devote to such silly things as Sputniks, rocket to the moon, and what have you, while their professors would be so busy preparing vague and somewhat misinformed "Notes on the News" they would certainly not have the leisure for scientific invention.

Of course, there is the bare, the hideous, possibility that some misguided Russian scientist might convert the great volume of hot air emitted by our politicians into the propellant still more powerful than that used to dispatch Sputnik II into outer space, but that is a studied risk we should not hesitate to take in these distracting times.

DECEMBER NEWS ITEMS

December 7ᵗʰ. **Armed small groups are taking many Dutch assets in Indonesia.** Over 100 trading ships have been detained in ports, **the Dutch population of 50,000 there has been ordered to leave at once**, and dozens of Banks and large corporations have been seized. The Government is doing nothing to stop the takeovers.

December 7ᵗʰ. **NSW has suffered in the last month from severe bushfires.** Last week, 150 houses were burned to the ground in the Blue Mountains, west of Sydney, bringing the total for a month to 250….

Sydney has introduced new control measures. They include the a ban on **striking of a match outdoors to light a cigarette**, and the **banning of candles at Christmas carols**. These measures will remain in force indefinitely, though some of them could be relaxed if decent rain falls soon.

Men who default on their alimony payments are sent to prison. At the moment, those in Sydney jails are being sent to the region of the new Warragamba Dam, and made to cut down trees. They are paid 10 shillings a week to do this….

The average adult male worker is paid about 40 times this sum. The public is outraged at this low rate of payment. It is argued that these men are not criminals, and should not be forced to do labour….

As well, it is argued, that if they were paid a decent wage, it could be used to reduce their alimony backlog. Finally, it is argued, that men in prison cannot earn their normal wage, and so they slip further behind in their alimony. Maybe the projected reforms to the divorce law will fix some of this.

Australia still rides on the sheep's back. Well, more or less. Wool is still our major export, and variations in the size of the clip and the prices gained are felt throughout the nation. This year, the clip was down 6 per cent because of droughts, but good prices made up for this. So that **it is the second biggest wool cheque we have ever received**. This has meant that 1957 has been **a prosperous year for the nation**, and that Federal budgetary moves have not been a worry.

December 12th. **The liner *Strathaird* left London for Australia with 1,278 passengers.** Nothing unusual about that. **Could be a nice, pleasant trip....**

But wait a minute. 500 of these are children from migrant families, and are aged 12 or under. This is the largest number of children ever carried out of Britain on the one ship, and **one English newspaper described it dramatically as a "hell ship."**

The Indonesian government has accepted it has a problem. When armed partisans took over Dutch enterprises, **it did nothing to stop them**. Now the penny is dropping, and it is realising **that it needs foreign capital, and foreign banks, and foreign workers who can manage the economy....**

It is not reversing the takeovers, but it is starting to talk about **compensation and slowing the deportations**. Maybe some sense will prevail. **But not in this book.**

TOP POP TUNES

Just Walking in the Rain	Johnnie Ray
Round and Round	Perry Como
Around The World	Bing Crosby
Singing The Blues	Guy Mitchell
Love Letters In The Sand	Pat Boone
A White Sport Coat	Marty Robbins
Young Love	Tab Hunter
Cindy, Oh Cindy	Eddie Fisher
Wonderful! Wonderful!	Johnny Mathis
Maryanne	The Easy Riders
Dianna	Paul Anka
Tammy	Debbie Reynolds
Hey There	Rosemary Clooney

TOP ACTORS AND FILMS

12 Angry Men	Henry Fonda, Lee J Cobb
Paths of Glory	Kirk Douglas
Sweet Smell of Success	Burt Lancaster, Tony Curtis
The River Kwai	Alex Guinness
The Shiralee	Peter Finch, Dana Wilson
Robbery Under Arms	Peter Finch, Ronald Lewis
Witness for Prosecution	Tyrone Power, Dietrich
A Face in the Crowd	Andy Griffith, Pat Neal
An Affair to Remember	Cary Grant, Deborah Kerr
Funny Face	Audrey Hepburn, Fred Astaire

ACADEMY AWARDS:

Best actor:	Yul Brynner (King and I)
Best Actress	Ingrid Bergman (Anastasia)

LUNG CANCER CAUSE?

Scientists and medical authorities in Britain and the USA were **beginning** to suspect that there was a strong link between smoking tobacco and various forms of lung cancer. Such news was not welcome to the tobacco companies, so there were many studies being initiated to find the truth. Or, in some cases, to obscure the truth.

On balance, the jury was still out. No one could say for sure if there was a link, and if so, how strong the link was. In Britain, say, the individual smoker found it hard to give up smoking on the conflicting information. Nearly all, at this stage, strongly influenced by tobacco adverts, decided there was no chance that **they** would fall prey to cancer, and kept puffing away with no qualms.

In Australia we, in our wonderful insular way, were not taking much notice of what was happening overseas. Thus our discussions were less scientific, and more emotional.

Letters, (Miss) N Williams. The individual may choose to smoke or not to smoke. Few indeed have a choice between living in cities, bombarded by cancer-forming substance in every breath, and living in the clean air of the country. Country jobs, especially for women, are neither plentiful nor well-paid; accommodation is no less difficult to find than in the city; amenities and amusements do not compare favourably.

It would, of course, be too much to expect our governments, local, State, or Federal, to act on city air pollution as the cause not only of lung cancer, chronic bronchitis, asthma, sinus and antrum inflammation, and other respiratory troubles, but also of thousands of pounds damage annually to paintwork, metal, furnishings, and clothing. Vested interests in factories and motor cars, Government enterprise in power-houses and diesel omnibuses, might be put to considerable expense in the suppression of atmospheric poisoning.

It is far simpler and less politically dangerous to attack ineffectually the pleasures of the individual citizen (employing his own tax money for the purpose), and then blame him for falling ill when he prefers present pleasure to future welfare.

Incidentally, to forestall the inevitable counter-attack, I am neither an employee nor a shareholder in any tobacco enterprise. I am, however, a moderate smoker and intend to remain so, whether living in city or country.

But if I were offered a well-paid country job, with accommodation of decent standard, I should very readily quit the filthy air of this city.

Letters, D J Halliday. Now that the British Government has officially taken notice of the dangers of smoking, and it has been suggested that our Australian authorities might do the same, may I urge the same subject on the attention of our Railways Department?

I suggest that the comfort of non-smoking passengers might be increased if three cars, instead of two, were provided for their use on suburban trains. There must be many non-smokers who travel **in smoking cars** for lack of other accommodation.

Then, too, our schoolchildren are not likely to be impressed with advice on non-smoking suggested when they see that in practice little provision is made for non-smokers, and they themselves travel to and from school in smoking compartments because there is insufficient accommodation otherwise.

Letters, R K Rae. The air pollution of modern cities, which Miss N V Williams so rightly deplores in her letter, has not increased significantly during the last 20 or 30 years; it is a constant factor. On the other hand there is incontrovertible evidence that the smoking of cigarettes has increased greatly.

Assuming then, as we must, that the air we breathe and the tobacco we smoke both contain carcinogens, surely it is logical to blame the increased consumption of cigarettes for any possible harmful effect.

It would seem that our greatly maltreated lungs can and do adapt themselves to receiving daily, from the contaminated air, a certain maximal amount of carcinogens without serious damage; if, by excessive smoking, we increase this amount then, in some cases, the lung tissue gives up the struggle, and cancer develops.

Of course, the individual may choose to smoke or not to smoke, but I for one object to the high-pressure propaganda of the tobacco interests from which it is impossible to escape – in the Press, on television, and even in the newsreel theatres. This propaganda aims at making our young people believe that is "smart" to smoke.

For the above reasons, I am in favour of Government counter-propaganda, not for the sake of the older people, but for the welfare of our children and future generations.

Comment.   I can recall a conversation I had 50 years later with smokers who were adamant that smoking was not related to cancers of the lung. They rolled out the old familiar arguments. Cigarette smoking was a lot safer than the roll-your-own of yesteryear, they said. It was not safe to use old newspapers to roll-your-own, but the special rice paper made the big difference. Pipes added an extra level of safety. The old practice of adding saltpeter had stopped. Filters on cigarettes made them perfectly safe. **Then the**

ultimate argument. Old Bill has smoked two packets a day for 100 years, and he is as fit as a fiddle.

What can you say in the face of all this logic? It was my turn to shrug my shoulders and say **"Silly old buggers."**

NEWS FROM AMERICA

A Press item appeared under the heading *America Swept by Credit Cards Fad*. It recounted, with some feeling of dismay and wonder, that thousands of Americans are turning from money to **credit cards** in transacting their everyday business.

It described how an American can go for a holiday without a penny in his pocket, tip a waiter, repair his yacht, or send his son to school. They can go to the movies and charge up their candy and popcorn.

Oil companies are issuing such cards, so that a motorist can travel the highways and byways of the country, having the car serviced, oiled and gassed up without once touching a penny in cash.

Comment. These Americans and their love of novelties! In a few years, these people will sit back and wonder at their own foolishness. **Credit cards indeed!**

THE BODKIN CRISIS

Bodkins are so familiar to you that I do not need to tell you of their many uses. But I do need to tell you that there is a shortage developing, and that something needs to be done about this.

Letters, A F Wilson. Our shops are not unusual in being heavily supplied with goods for the betterment of living. They overflow with washing machines, radiograms and every shop sells everything. The music shop sells washing machines and the toy shop sells pianos. The general stores are choked with tools and plastics.

So I hopefully asked at several stores: "Have you a bodkin?" But no.

At another store the young girl looked quite frightened and asked: "What is it?" I resisted the mad impulse to explain that in my youth we used it to thread ribbons in our camisoles, and said it was for the purpose of weaving the toe of a hand-knitted sock.

But we were not speaking the same language and generations apart. "No, no bodkin!"

Comment. I can't believe that a shop in 1957 does not carry bodkins. What is the world coming to?

COMMENTS ON CHURCHES AND REDS

When I get to the end of a book, I like to get off the fence I have been sitting on, and write freely about a few` things that have stirred me a little over the year. So now I will indulge myself, and talk about Churches and the Reds.

This year, there were a lot of situations that the clergy got involved in. It was nice to see them responding publicly, in contrast to times in the past when they stuck their heads in the sand, and beat their breasts, and said that God knew they were right and that was all that mattered.

So, now they came out of their shells. But they came out in a manner that must have shocked their congregations. Time and time again, their Letters were full of invective and spite against other branches of the Christian church. They were irrelevant and petty. Where logic and reasoning would have been welcome, they instead as a last resort quoted some obscure passage from the Bible as if that clinched all matters. They showed none of the Christian values of tolerance and steadiness that they constantly espouse.

In short, those who responded via Letters made a poor showing. It is a consolation to me, and I know it will be to all readers, to realise that the vast majority who did not respond would have been just as disappointed as I was.

Now for the Reds. Around the world, and in this nation, they were agitating to gain as much power and control as they could. In doing this, in Australia, they came under fire from the Liberals, the newspapers, the Churches, and many fine public figures. In short, **they had a bad Press. In fact, a very bad Press.** And this went on from 1945, when the Russians switched from being goodies to baddies, right up to the present.

Little wonder then that many of our worthy citizens had come to believe that everything about Russia was bad. In terms of the Letters I have reviewed for this book, it was possible to write Letters to the Papers, and mention the Reds, and this was taken as proof positive that the counter position taken was the correct one. It was just the same as with the churches above. For those writers, all they had to do to win a point of contention was to quote from the Bible. For the anti-Communist writers, all **they** had to do was to mention Russia or the Reds, or Hungary, and suddenly the opposition was supposed to slink away.

Clearly, in my view, both of these situations needed more thought. I think that there are plenty of arguments, **for and against and neither**, that can be made on **every** issue. But one that should **not** be used is the chanting of slogans based on the mindless acceptance of oft-repeated non-arguments.

SUMMING UP 1957

After I have now alienated half my readers, let me review the year of 1957. The most spectacular event was the launching of the two sputniks. The world was captivated, and if the dog had come down in one piece, the Cold War might have ended overnight with Russia the undisputed champion of everything. This did not happen.

One thing that **did** happen was the almost perceptible growth in **the support for the Aborigines**. As more people became aware of their plight, so more of the population wanted to **help** them. As I watched that feeling grow, I thrilled that so many good people, when confronted by misery, were anxious to do what they could to improve matters.

It might surprise you to know that I was proud to be part of **that** Australia. I know there was, and still is, a great deal to be done, but in those early days of an Aboriginal renaissance, to realise that so many people felt as I did was a great feeling. None of us had, **or have**, the slightest idea of what can be done to improve things, **but the recognition of the need was a good place to start from**.

As for other events, I delighted in the decision to build the Opera House. This was pretty brave, and the use of Opera House lotteries to do so was the type of political risk that few politicians are prepared to take.

Then there were other events that are worthy of mention. The eating of the roo by a crocodile rated highly, as did the side-show put on by Porky. The idea of playing music to mollify sharks has not, I feel, been tested thoroughly enough.   But somehow it might tie in with the placing of loudspeakers at intervals along our beaches, playing *muzac*. It would be a pity to see such a good idea go away just because everyone would hate it.

As to the future, I happen to know that this great little nation will be **blessed with peace** for at least the next 60 years. That will not be **perfect** peace because the Vietnam War in the middle of the next decade will kill some of our best. But, apart from that folly and tragedy, we will have peace. And I happen to know that for most of us, we will have **prosperity and harmony** that is scarcely ever seen in any other part of the world. Even our unfortunates will have a security blanket that is as good or better than any other .

So, I say, our future holds peace and prosperity for **a full life-tim**e. If you were lucky enough to be born into that year, I congratulate you, and **hope that your good luck stays with you for the rest of your long life**.

Born in 1943?
What else happened?
Australian Social History

Ron Williams

In 1943, a Jap invasion was no longer on the cards. But Chifley liked butter, clothing, and meat rationing. And the blackout covers on all windows could be removed. Though, he added a week later, that they had to go up again. Zoot suits were now for the wearing, fights in city pubs were very popular especially if they involved US servicemen.

Born in 1944?
What else happened?
Australian Social History

Ron Williams

In 1944, the Japs in the Pacific and the Nazis in Europe was just about beaten. Sydney was invaded by rats, and there were lots of Yankee soldiers in all our cities, and a few of them were not hated. Young girls were being corrupted by the Yanks and by war-time freedom, and clergy were generous with their advice to them.

****

Chrissy and birthday books for Mum and Dad and Aunt and Uncle and cousins and family and friends and work and everyone else.

Don't forget a good read and chuckle for yourself.

Born in 1949?
What else happened?
Australian Social History
Ron Williams

In 1949, the Reds in China could rest from their Long March, and the Reds in Australia took a battering in the pits. The rabbits ruled the paddocks, and some Churches suffered from outbreaks of dirty dancing and housie. Immigration Minister Calwell crudely enforced the White Australia Policy, so that huge crowds on the beaches were nervous about getting a tan. There was plenty of petrol for motorists in NZ and Britain, but not here, so Bob Menzies cruised to another election win over Labor.

****

AVAILABLE FROM ALL GOOD BOOK STORES AND NEWSAGENTS